Fundamentals of Agricultural Extension

Dr. Utpal Barman
Assistant Professor (S.G)

Dr. Rajendra Kumar Talukdar
Professor and Head

Dr. Prasanta Mishra
Assistant Professor (S.G)

Mr. Sajib Borua
Assistant Professor (S.G)
Department of Extension Education
Faculty of Agriculture, Assam Agricultural University
Jorhat, Assam

AGROBIOS

Published by:
AGROBIOS (INDIA)
Agro House, Behind Nasrani Cinema
Chopasani Road, Jodhpur 342 003
Website: *www.agroacademics.com*
E. mail: *agrobiosindia@gmail.com*

ISBN No.: 978-81-7754-442-3 (HB)

Published by: Dr. Updesh Purohit for Agrobios (India), Jodhpur
Laser Typeset at: Yashee Computers, Jodhpur
Cover Design by: Shyam
Printed at: Agrobios Digitals, Jodhpur

Preface

This book is prepared for the undergraduate agricultural source of 'Dimension of Agricultural Extension' as per revised curriculum in Extension Education for B.Sc. (Agri) degree programme. There is a number of good books on Extension Education. But it was observed that students face difficulty to find one that encompasses the new course contents in its length and breadth. The book already published contains the contents in different depths without emphasizing the importance and stress to be attached to such course contents. No books extensively deal with the new course. So, to solve this problem of undergraduate students studying under the agricultural system, this textbook has prepared. It is expected that the book will meet the requirements of the new system with the fullest satisfaction to the students.

Agricultural Education has undergone a change in its contents, approaches, emphasis and even methodology. As a vast research knowledge is being generated, new areas of learning in agriculture are being explored. Teaching approaches are constantly modified, farmers' orientation is getting changed; professional's challenge is increasing so new items are being added with every passing ear in the Agricultural Education system. Agricultural course curricula are now prepared under the instruction of ICAR, New Delhi to maintain uniformity in contents all thought the country b a group of experts drawn from all over the country. The 4th Dean's committee recommended the present course curricula and this book is prepared as per the new contents. Some additional but important contents are also included in the book for the benefit of the students, particularly for competitive examination.

The authors express their sense of gratitude to their colleagues for providing valuable suggestions for preparing the textbook.

Authors' thanks also go to Ms. Maya Mahanta, Mr. Prabin Kalita, Mr. Maheswar Dutta, Mr. Prafulla Bora, Mr. Rajen Gogoi and Mr. Manik Bordoloi for their valuable help. They also thank Agrobios (India) for agreeing to publish the book. At last, they also welcome constructive criticism from teachers, students etc. for improving the textbook in the near future.

Authors

Contents

CHAPTER 1

Education: Concept and Types

1.0 OBJECTIVES

This unit seeks to help the students to understand the concept and meaning of education. The unit will enable the students to comprehend different types of education and their characteristics. After completion of the unit, students will be able to:

- Define education
- List different types of education
- Differentiate different types of education by following their characteristics
- Recall the key elements of non-formal education
- Mention the learning processes of non formal education
- Tell the dont's of non-formal education

1.1 INTRODUCTION

Before knowing about the concept of 'extension education,' it is essential to know the concept of 'education'. Some terms like 'informal education', 'non-formal education', 'formal education' etc. should also be clarified before understanding the term 'extension education'. This unit will help the student to understand some concept and terms related to education.

1.2 CONCEPT AND MEANING OF EDUCATION

The word education comes from the Latin e-ducere meaning "to lead out". Education is the process of bringing desirable change into the behaviour of human beings. It is the process of imparting or acquiring knowledge and habits through instruction or study. When learning is progressing towards goals that have been established in accordance with a philosophy which has been defined for, and is understood by the learner, it is called education (Dahama and Bhatnagar, 1991). Education is the process of developing capabilities of the individuals so that they can adequately respond to their situations (Roy, 1996).

1.3 TYPES OF EDUCATION

Coombs and Ahmed (1974) mentioned three types of education and drew a distinction between them as follows:

1. Informal Education
2. Formal Education
3. Non-formal Education

1.3.1 Informal education

It is a life long process by which every person acquires and accumulates knowledge, skills and insights from daily experience and exposure to the environment, at home, at play, at work etc. from parents, friends, e.g. child learning to eat from mother (Coombs and Ahmed, 1974). Informal Education is as follows:

- Life long process
- Continuous
- Experiential

1.3.2 Formal education

It is highly institutionalised, chronologically graded and hierarchically structured 'education system (Coombs and Ahmed, 1974). e.g. School level to university level. According to Dahama and Bhatnagar (1991), formal education is basically uniform, subject-oriented, full time, sequential, leading to a degree, diploma, certificates etc. A formal education program is the process of training and developing people in knowledge, skills, mind, and character in a structured and certified programme (SIL International, 1999). Formal Education is:

- Institutionalised, means it is the activities of the formal institution which provides education. For example, school, college etc.

- Chronologically graded.
- Hierarchically structured means lower level (Primary) to higher level (University).

1.3.2 Non-formal education

It is an organised, systematic, educational activity carried on outside the framework of the formal system to provide selected types of learning to particular sub-groups in the population, adults as well as children according to their need (Coombs and Ahmed, 1974). Non-formal education is an instruction that is not obligatory and structured and is learned outside the context of a formal school (SIL International, 1999). Adult education and extension education are parts of non-formal education. Coombs and Ahmed (1974) group these approaches under four major categories:

i) the extension approach,
ii) the training approach,
iii) the cooperative self- help approach, and
iv) the integrated development approach.

1.4 KEY ELEMENTS OF NON FORMAL EDUCATION

Etling, Radhakrishna and Bowen (1993) mentioned six key elements of non-formal education, which are given below:

- ***Non-formal education is learner-centred:*** It means that non-formal education should address the needs and interests of the learners. The curriculum should be prepared after analysing the practical need of the learners. The topic should not be imposed on the learner.
- ***There are variety, options and flexibility in the curriculum which are generated primarily by the learners:*** To address the varied requirements of the learners, the curriculum should have the options and should be flexible enough to accommodate required topics. The topic should be delivered by following varieties of methods that will attract attention and captivates the interest of the learners.
- ***Informal human relationships are essential:*** Informal human relation between teachers and learners will help to create a

non-threatening atmosphere which facilitates learning. It will also provide scope to the learner to share their experiences.

- ***Reliance on local resources and available resources are deployed efficiently:*** The learner will learn easily if local resources could be used during the learning process as these are familiar to the learner. It will also reduce the cost of learning. So local resources should be deployed efficiently.
- ***Educational content and methodology are directly related to learners' lifestyles and have immediate use:*** Adults will not learn for future use. The learning should have immediate utility for them. So, the contents should be directly related to their lifestyles, livelihood and have immediate use. The methodologies followed for teaching should also be compatible with their lifestyles and immediate need.
- ***Less bureaucratic and more decentralisation allows local approaches to the solution of local problems:*** The person who is facing the problem is the right person to understand the problems. So, it is better to encourage him or her to suggest remedy instead of giving the same by the extension worker in a bureaucratic manner. People will come out to discuss their problems in a democratic setup where everybody will get an equal chance to speak or participate. So, non-formal education should be conducted in a democratic way.

1.5 LEARNING PROCESSES OF NON FORMAL EDUCATION

According to Dahama and Bhatnagar (1991), learning in a non-formal education programme takes place through:

- ***Democratic discussion and dialogue:*** Learning in non-formal education will take place if there is scope for equal participation for each learner. Everybody should get the opportunity to express his or her views.
- ***Critical analysis of factors in the environment:*** Learning will not take place in isolation. Different factors of the environment will play a major role in this regards. So, all the factors in the environment like socio-economic, cultural, physical etc. should be listed with the active participation of adults and critically analysed for their impacts.

- ***Self-analysis and reflection leading to understanding:*** Learners are also knowledgeable and experienced. So, after getting the information, they will critically analyse these based on their own knowledge and experience and try to comprehend the information in relation to their situation.
- ***Autonomous selection of information:*** Based on their needs and interest, the learner will select the desired information. This selection is autonomous in nature. If it is imposed, then learning will not take place.
- ***Action programmes and community activities:*** People will also learn through participation in different activities. When the community actively participates in an activity, then it will build the confidence of the learner, and that will help them learn easily.
- ***Training in practical skills:*** Learners will develop skill quickly if they are provided with opportunities to practice.
- ***Sharing experiences:*** Adult learners have lots of experience, and they want to share those things with others. If they get the opportunities to share their experiences than they will learn quickly.
- ***Relating education to life, social and work experiences:*** Adults have the orientation to learning. But this should be related to their life, social obligations and job. They will not learn only for the sack of learning.

1.6 DONT'S OF NON FORMAL EDUCATION

While implementing the learning programmes, some points should be avoided in case of non-formal education to enhance effectiveness. For example, non-formal education should not be:

- **Authoritarian and imposed:** In case of non-formal education, the instructor should not give instruction or impose any ideas to the students who are generally adult learners. The teacher should act as a facilitator rather than an expert. They will learn those subject which is need-based and relevant to them. If the matter is imposed by the instructor, they will resist learning. The entire learning process should be in a democratic manner. Lerner, in the case of non-formal education, simply rejects the authoritarian types of the instructor, and they will not learn anything from him or her. Learning should not be one way and instructive.

- **Abstract and theoretical:** The topic of non-formal education should be practical in nature. It should be immediately used by the learner. The adult will not learn for future use. If the topic has a bearing on immediate actions or devoid of any practical utility, then they will not learn that type of topic.
- **Mechanical and routine:** Non-formal education should not follow the style of formal education, which is the almost mechanical and routine type of works. The topic must link with the learner's needs and interest and how it will solve their problems. Simple one-way classroom teaching is not sufficient to teach the adult learner through non-formal education. The scope should be given to the learner to share their experience during the learning process.
- **Unrelated to the concerns and interest of learners**: In case of non-formal education, learners are mostly adults. One of the important characteristics of adult learning is that they will learn only those things which are need-based and interesting for them. If the topic is not addressing their concern, then they will not learn those things.

1.7 SUMMARY

In this unit, we studied that education is the process of bringing desirable changes in the behaviour of human beings. There are different types of education like informal, formal and non-formal education. There are six key elements of non-formal education. Learning in case of non-formal education takes place in different ways. In the case of non-formal education, a teacher should not impose the topic to the learner. He should act as a facilitator rather than an expert. The topic should be need-based and should have practical utility for the learner.

1.8 KEYWORDS

- **Education:** Education is the process of bringing desirable change into the behaviour of human beings. It is the process of developing capabilities of the individuals so that they can adequately respond to their situations.

- **Informal education:** Life long process by which every person acquires and accumulates knowledge, skills and insights from daily experience and exposure to the environment at home, at play, at work etc.
- **Formal education:** It is highly institutionalised, chronologically graded and hierarchically structured education system.
- **Non-formal education:** It is an organised, systematic, educational activity carried on outside the framework of the formal system to provide selected types of learning to particular sub-groups in the population, adults, youths as well as children according to their need.

1.9 CHECK YOUR PROGRESS

1. What do you mean by 'education'? Explain different types of education with suitable example.
2. Describe the key elements of non-formal education.
3. Why non-formal education should be democratic in nature?
4. In non-formal education teacher should acknowledge the experience of the learners. Why?

CHAPTER 2

Concept of Extension Education

2.0 OBJECTIVES

This unit aims to help the students' understanding of the growth of extension education. The unit will enable the students to comprehend definitions, objectives, philosophy and principles of extension education and agricultural extension. It will also help the students to differentiate extension education from formal education. After completion of the unit, students will be able to

- State the growth of Extension Education
- Describe concept, meaning and definition of Extension Education and Agricultural Extension
- Differentiate extension, extension education and agricultural extension.
- List the objectives of Extension Education and Agricultural Extension
- State philosophy of Extension Education
- Describe the principles of Extension Education
- Differentiate extension education from formal education

2.1 INTRODUCTION

The word extension is derived from the Latin words ex means 'out', and 'tensio' means 'stretching". The extension is that type of education which is stretched out to people in the rural areas far and near, beyond the limits of the educational institutions while the formal type of education is usually confined within the four walls of the institute. Education is an integral part of the extension. Because of this, and because of the fact that extension is pursued in agriculture and many other disciplines to educate, motivate and change the behaviour of the people, this particular branch of science is also known as extension education (Roy, 1996).

2.2 GROWTH OF EXTENSION

Jones and Garforth (1997) mentioned that the use of the word "extension" derives from an educational development in England during the second half of the nineteenth century. Around 1850, discussions began in the two ancient universities of Oxford and Cambridge about how they could serve the educational needs, near to their homes, of the rapidly growing populations in the industrial, urban area. The actual use of the term 'extension' thus originated in England in 1866 with a system of university extension which was taken up first by Cambridge and Oxford Universities, and later by other educational institutions in England and in other Countries. The term 'extension education' was first used in 1873 by Cambridge University to describe this particular educational innovation (Swanson and Claar, 1984).

Jones and Garforth (1997) after collecting information from different sources reported some historical evidence of extension activities. This information is selectively mentioned in the following paragraphs.

According to them, the dissemination of relevant information and advice to farmers has a long history prior to the emergence of modem forms of agricultural extension in the nineteenth century. The first known example was in Mesopotamia around 1800 B.C. Archaeologists had unearthed clay tablets of the time on which were inscribed advice on watering crops and getting rid of rats - important for mitigating any potential loss of taxation revenue from farmers. Some hieroglyphs on Egyptian columns also gave advice on avoiding crop damage and loss of life from the Nile's floods. The earliest agricultural writings were written during the ancient Greek and Phoenician civilizations. From the second century B.C. to the fourth century A.D., several important Latin texts were written, frequently drawing on practical farming experience, which aimed to help Roman landowners to maintain and improve their estates and their revenues. At around the same period in imperial China, early forms of advancing and disseminating agricultural information also began. The support of relevant agricultural research and the dissemination of information and advice had begun by the late Han Dynasty (25-220 A.D.). The oldest fully surviving Chinese agricultural treatise is *Essential Techniques for the Peasantry,* dating from 535 A.D. It aimed to show landowners how to improve their farm management through the advice they gave to their tenants. The Sung and Yuan Dynasties (960-1368) were notable in organising and promoting agricultural research, extension work, and the teaching of agriculture and sericulture. It was facilitated by the invention of woodblock printing, which allowed agricultural treatises and practical handbooks to be widely distributed.

The first agricultural extension service of a modem kind came into existence as the result of the outbreak of potato blight in Europe in 1845. In Ireland, its effects were particularly severe because the peasant population relied on potatoes in their diet, and "the potato famine" persisted until 1851. The Earl of Clarendon, the British Viceroy to Ireland wrote a letter in 1847 to the President of the Royal Agricultural Improvement Society of Ireland. This letter urged the society to appoint itinerant lecturers to travel around the most distressed districts to inform and show small farmers how to improve their cultivation and how to grow nutritious root crops other than potatoes.

The potato famine also led to consideration being given in Württemberg to employing itinerant farm advisers, but the proposal failed to gain approval. However, from the mid-1850s, first, in Württemberg, Hesse, and western Prussia, itinerant agricultural teachers (*Wanderlehrer*) began to be appointed under the auspices of central agricultural societies. After some ten years, the system grew rapidly and became formalised. Normally, the *Wanderlehrer* spent the summer half of the year travelling around their districts giving talks, demonstrations, and advice to farmers; during the remainder of the year, they taught farmers' sons at winter agricultural schools. By the close of the nineteenth century, agricultural extension systems modelled to a considerable extent on the German *Wanderlehrer* had spread. Meanwhile, in France, the first national, wholly state-funded agricultural extension service was established in 1879.

In the United States and eastern Canada, agricultural societies had become common during the first half of the ninetieth century. However, two other developments after 1850 were of more significance to the evolution of agricultural extension in the United States. First was the Morrill Act of 1862, which established Land Grant Colleges. The second was the beginning at about the same time as the farmers' institute movement. These institutes organized one-or two-day (and later longer) meetings, which became popular after 1860, arranged by and for farmers. The visiting speakers at the institutes were largely professors at the state colleges of agriculture. Over the next forty years, these activities were influenced also by the university extension movement in Britain and the growing interest in adult self-improvement. The efforts were further stimulated by the formal establishment of experimental work at the state colleges of agriculture under the 1887 Hatch Act. In the United States, the colleges and their leading professors progressively took over the initiation and organization of the activity. This culminated in 1914 with the passage of the Smith-Lever Act, establishing the Cooperative Extension Service in the U.S.A.

Cooperative extension and home economics of U.S.A. is the first organised extension work in the world. It is a cooperative extension effort of local people of county government, the state through its land grant colleges and the federal government through a special unit in the U.S. Department of Agriculture. The extension system is educational in nature. It emphasises on grass root approach, democratic values, people's involvement and practical learning etc. Most of the developing countries, including India, borrowed the concept of extension work from the U.S.A.

A central department of agriculture was established in India after the 1866 Orissa famine, and the government of India soon after resolved to establish departments in each province. However, it was 1905 before a central government directive ordered every province to appoint a full-time director of agriculture who should organise agricultural research and demonstration farms with staff who could advise farmers. In India, Calcutta University was the first institute who started teaching extension education as an undergraduate course in 1950. It was started at the College of Agriculture, Jhargram. The first ever postgraduate course on extension education was started at Bihar Agricultural College, Sabour in 1955 and next at College of Agriculture, Nagpur in 1958. The first PhD programme in extension education was started at IARI, New Delhi in 1960 and next at Punjab Agricultural University in 1965. Indian Society of Extension Education was established on 22nd June 1964.

2.3 CONCEPT, MEANING AND DEFINITIONS OF EXTENSION, EXTENSION EDUCATION AND AGRICULTURAL EXTENSION

According to Ensminger (1957), the extension is education and that its purpose is to change the attitudes and practices of the people with whom the work is done. It means that extension changes the behaviour of the people with respect to attitude (mindset) and practices (habit)

The National Commission on Agriculture (1976) refers to extension as an out of school education and services for the members of the farm family and others directly or indirectly engaged in farm production to enable them to adopt improved practices in production, management, conservation and marketing. The Commission further stated that, agricultural extension is not only imparting knowledge and securing adoption of a particular improved practice but also aims at changing the outlook of the farmers to the point where they will be receptive to, and on their own initiative, continuously seek means of improving their farm occupation, home and family life in totality. This definition mentioned that extension is a non-formal education for the betterment of the farming community.

According to Bhatnagar and Desai (1987) extension is to bring the desired changes in the behaviour- knowledge, skills, attitude, understanding, goals and confidence of the people through mutual learning. Here extension is a two ways educational process.

The extension involves the conscious use of communication of information to help people from sound opinions and make good decisions. (van den Ban and Hawkins, 1988). Here the role of extension is information provider for better decision making.

Kelsey and Hearne (1954) defined extension as an out of school system of education in which the adults and young people learn by doing the job themselves. Here the principle is learning by doing.

Mosher (1979), however, feels that the concept of the extension has to go beyond education in developing countries where the most important need of the farmers is not just to make better use of the resources already available with them, but to get access to one or more specific resources. The National Commission on Agriculture (1976) was, however of the view that extension is basically education and preparation for change.

Legans (1961) conceptualized extension education as an applied science consisting of content derived from research, accumulated field experiences and relevant principles drawn from the behavioural sciences synthesised with useful technology into a body of philosophy, principles, content and methods focused on the problems of out of school education for adult and youth. This definition indicates that extension education is an applied science and its contents are collected from research findings, experiences generated from field activities and some principles are also drawn from behavioural sciences since extension deals with a human being. These contents are than synthesise with useful technologies to develop its own philosophy, principles, content etc. to solve the problems of adult and youth throughout of school education.

In most of the countries, extension education is known as agricultural extension, because extension services in these countries are mainly concerned with the development of agriculture. When work is done to help housewives, it is known as home-economic extension or home science extension. If it is concerned with animal, it becomes a veterinary extension. Otherwise, the main meaning is the same for all cases.

Liniger (1953) stated that agricultural extension is helping farmers to help themselves. It indicates that extension helps the farmers to become self-dependent.

Having studied the meaning, concept and definitions of extension, extension education and agricultural extension, another issue should be clear in the distinction between the terms *extension* and *extension education*. Rolling (1982) makes the distinction between extension and extension education quite clear. According to him, extension refers to the actual work done by professional extension agents at various levels of management, while extension education refers to the body of knowledge concerning that work practice. He says that the distinction is comparable to the one between the trainer and trainer of trainers. The terms 'extension' and 'transfer of technology' are also often used interchangeably, but the two are different. While the extension is an educational process, transfer of technology includes the additional functions of supplies and services (Misra, 1990). Agricultural extension is an essential and major part of technology transfer, but the terms are not synonymous (Swanson and Clarr, 1984). Transfer of technology is a much wider term than extension.

Regarding 'extension', 'rural extension', and 'agricultural extension', the extension is a wider term. According to (Swanson and Clarr, 1984), an extension can be used successfully by different types of organizations to reach different groups of people with different messages. The rural extension can cover an aspect or all aspects of rural development, including agricultural extension. Agricultural extension is the narrowest in scope among all the three concepts of extension, rural extension and agricultural extension. Swanson and Clarr (1984) say that the term, agricultural extension, narrows the focus and defines the areas to which the extension process is applied.

2.4 OBJECTIVES OF EXTENSION

An objective is "an expression of the end or direction of movement towards which efforts are directed". The broad objectives of extension education are to bring about desirable changes in the behaviour of the people. More specifically, the objectives of the extension are –

1. ***To assist people in discovering and analyzing their problems and identifying the felt needs:*** Instead of identifying and analysing the problems and felt needs of people, the extension helps them to do so. It facilitates proper identification of problems and selecting their solution because people know their situation very well than the extension workers.
2. ***To develop leadership among people and help them in***

organizing groups to solve their problems: When people work in the group, then it is easy for them to solve their problems because they can share their knowledge, experiences, skills and resources etc. in groups. For organising people to work through the group, we need leaders. Here extension helps to develop leadership among people.

3. ***To disseminate research information of economic and practical importance in a way people would be able to understand and use:*** Technologies are developed by scientists and generally contain technical terms which may not be understandable to the people. So, extension disseminates that research information in simple language so that people can understand the same. When they will understand then only they can decide to adopt it.
4. ***To assist people in mobilizing and utilizing the resources which they have and which they need from outside*:** Extension helps the people to identify resources needed to solve their programme. It facilitates to analyse which resources can be found locally and which can be brought from outside. If resources are available locally, then it is easy for them to solve the problem without depending on others.
5. ***To collect and transmit feedback information for solving management problems:*** Extension worker collects feedback from clients and disseminates the same to scientists so that they can solve the management problems. It is generally a difficult task for researchers to collect feedback regularly from the field. So, extension collects the feedback for them and transmits to the researcher for further necessary action.

National Commission on Agriculture (1976) stated that agricultural extension aims at improving the efficiency of the human capital in an effort to rapidly increase the rate of agricultural production. Simply developing technology is not sufficient to increase agricultural production. One major factor for increasing production is the human capital that will use the technology. So, we have to give due attention to improve the efficiency of human capital. Otherwise, they will not be able to utilise the technology in the right way.

According to Van den Ban and Hawkins (1988), the extension is a process which helps farmers:

- To become aware of problems that arise in such analyses,
- Increase knowledge and develops insight into problems and helps to structure their existing knowledge
- Help farmers acquire specific knowledge related to a certain problem, solutions and their consequences so they can act on possible alternatives.
- To make a responsible choice, which, in their opinion, is optimal for their situation
- Increases farmers motivation to implement their choices and
- Helps to evaluate and improve their own opinion-forming and decision-making skills.

2.5 OBJECTIVES OF AGRICULTURAL EXTENSION

The objectives of the extension are held equally fit for agricultural extension too. However, IGNOU (1992) mentioned some specific objectives of agricultural extension, which are given below:

- To educate farmers about farming innovations and prepare them for change and development.
- To provide improved technology, information and skills to farmers for increasing agricultural and livestock production, and productivity.
- To give feedback from the field to the research stations on the application of technology generated by them.
- To assist farmers in getting access to services and supplies, credit and marketing, and help them develop resources like land and water.
- To help farmers in making effective farm management decisions.
- To help in increased production of particular commodities, overcome their shortage or meet the developmental needs of the region or country.
- To encourage, motivate and help the farmers at times of depression, especially in the early stages of agricultural development.

- To help farmers to organize themselves for increased efficiency in processing and marketing of farm produce.

2.6 PHILOSOPHY OF EXTENSION EDUCATION

According to Kelsey and Hearne (1967), the basic philosophy of extension education is to teach people how to think not what to think. That means extension education teach people about the procedure of thinking so that they can be able to think properly to solve their problem. Bhatnagar and Desai (1987) also mentioned some philosophy of extension education. They said that the extension is an educational, cooperative, collaborative, democratic, persuasive and never-ending process that generates harmony, leadership, effective communication, participation and involvement of the people in organising self-help activities and projects. It is a system of learning by doing, seeing is believing at an individual level and mutual- learning at group level amongst professionals and target beneficiaries, resulting in a high degree of rapport and empathy.

Horton (1952) describes four principles which make the philosophy of extension. These are:

1. the individual is supreme in a democracy
2. the home is the fundamental unit in a civilization
3. the family is the first training group of the human race, and
4. the foundation of any permanent civilization must rest on the partnership of man and land.
5. According to Ensminger (1962), the philosophies of the extension are:
   a) It is an educational process
   b) The extension is working with men and women, young people, boys and girls to answer their needs and their wants.
   c) The extension is helping people to help themselves.
   d) The extension is learning by doing and seeing is believing
   e) The extension is the development of individuals, their leaders, their society and their world as a whole.
   f) The extension is working together to expand the welfare

and happiness of people.

g) The extension is working in harmony with the culture of the people

h) The extension is a living relationship, respect and trust for each other.

i) The extension is a two-way channel

j) The extension is a continuous, educational process

Dahama (1965) also mentioned some philosophies of extension. These are:

1. Self-help
2. People are the greatest resources
3. It is a cooperative effort
4. It has its foundation in democracy
5. It involves a two-way channel of knowledge and experience
6. It is based on creating interest by seeing and doing
7. Voluntary, cooperative participation in the programme
8. Persuasion and education of the people
9. The programme is based on the attitudes and values of the people
10. It is a never-ending process.

2.7 PRINCIPLES OF EXTENSION EDUCATION

The principle can be defined as a statement of policy to guide decisions and actions in a proper manner. The most important principles of extension education are given below.

1. **Principle of grass root approach:** Extension work must be started from the grass root level of the clients. It should be started where the people are. Things must be spread from below. The objectives of the programme should be formulated after studying the situation, needs, interest and problems of the people. People's participation is more assured if it starts from below.
2. **Principle of cooperation and participation:** Cooperation is the basis for the existence of extension service. The extension is an educational process of bringing desirable change into the behaviour of human beings. People are more likely to change

their behaviour when they have participated in planning the programme. People know their situation very well than the extension personnel. So, when they get a chance to plan the programme, then they will participate actively. They become dynamic if they take a decision concerning their own needs. So, extension follows the principle of cooperation and allows the people to participate in the planning and implementing the development programme.

3. **Principle of voluntary education:** Educational process of extension is voluntary in nature. Here, the participation of people is voluntary. People will participate in the programme if it begins with the needs and interest of the people. They will participate voluntarily if they get convinced about the benefits of the new programme.
4. **Principle of cultural difference:** Culture is the changing pattern of learned behaviour. It is shared by members of society and transmitted from one generation to the next generation. So, culture varies between members of different societies. There is a cultural difference between the extension agents and the farmers. Again, different farmers have different culture. The differences may exist in their habits, customs, values and attitudes etc. Extension work must accept these cultural differences and work accordingly. It must be carried out in harmony with the cultural pattern of the people to make it more successful.
5. **Principles of indigenous knowledge:** Every community has its indigenous knowledge systems. These are developed through generations of work experience and problem-solving in their specific situations. The indigenous knowledge systems encompass all aspects of life, and people consider it essential for their survival. Extension worker should not reject this knowledge as outdated. The extension worker should try to understand them in a related context and analyse their influence on the members of the community. There are numbers of indigenous knowledge which are very good even for today. So, while recommending a new technology, the extension worker must consider this point.
6. **Principle of interest and needs:** Extension work starts with

people's interest and needs. The extension agents should identify the needs and interest of the people. He should not impose his own needs and interests as those of the people. When extension work is based on people's needs and interest, then people's active participation will be more. In that situation, extension work will be successful.

7. **Principle of learning by doing:** Only receiving the knowledge is not sufficient to make the learning permanent and perfect. When people get involved in actually doing the work, then only learning will be perfect. Experience is important in learning. Learning by doing is most effective in changing people's behaviour. The action builds confidences.
8. **Principle of whole family approach:** Extension work aims at the development of the society. Family is the primary unit of society. So, for developing society, one should develop the family first. In a family, women and young members also influence a lot in decision making. Therefore, they should also be the target for extension work. When the whole family develops economically and socially, then society will be developed too. Therefore, an extension, the whole family approach is adopted involving men, women and youth members.
9. **Principle of leadership:** There are different types of leaders in society, and they have a good influence on the members. Some are a leader in agricultural aspects; some are on culture and so on. Generally, extension workers are cosmopolite in nature. They do not belong to the same social system of the clients. So, identifying different types of leaders and working through them is essential for them. With the help of these leaders, the extension worker can approach the target group easily. If local leaders oppose a programme, then it is very difficult to implement. So, local leaders and legitimisation by them are essential for the success of a programme. Extension worker should develop leadership traits among the people so that they can take the initiative for development. The leaders may be trained and developed to act as a vehicle of change in the villages.
10. **Principles of adaptability:** The people, their resources, problems and constraints vary from place to place and time

to time. Therefore extension work and extension teaching methods must be flexible, and it should suit the local conditions. If it is not suited in the local conditions, then it will not get the desired results.

11. **Principle of evaluation:** Evaluation means measuring something against some predetermined criteria. It helps extension workers to find out their own strength and weakness and prevents stagnation. Evaluation should be a continuous method for an extension. Evaluation helps the extension workers to increase the speed of achievements in the desired direction by strengthening the strong points and eliminating the weaknesses.
12. **Principle of satisfaction:** Satisfaction brings motivation. So, people's satisfaction is important in extension work. Extension work should produce satisfying results for the people. Satisfying results facilitate learning. Once satisfied, people will easily motivate to seek further help from the extension agencies.

2.8 DIFFERENCE BETWEEN FORMAL EDUCATION AND EXTENSION EDUCATION

Formal education and extension education are two different types of education. Dahama and Bhatnagar (1991) mentioned some differences in formal education and extension education, which are given below.

Sl. No.	Formal education	Extension education
1	Starts from a theoretical or conceptual framework and leads to practical or actual field work	It is practical, field and farmer's problem-oriented thus starts from a practical and develops into a theoretical or basic understanding
2	Has fixed curriculum	No fixed curriculum
3	Homogeneous audience	Heterogeneous audience
4	Teaching is curriculum centred	Mostly need-based and problem-oriented
5	Strict adherence to institutional norms and no free choice for the learners	Freedom and choice of subject matter left to the learners

2.9 SUMMARY

In this unit, we studied that extension activities were carried out even in the ancient period. The term 'extension' and 'extension education' were originated in England in 1866 and 1873 respectively. The extension is an educational process. The objective of extension education is to bring about desirable changes in the behaviour of the people. Philosophy of extension indicates that it is learning by doing, seeing is believing and helping people to help themselves etc. The extension follows the numbers of principles. At last, we learn that the extension of education is different from formal education in many ways.

2.10 KEYWORDS

- **Extension:** It is education and that its purpose is to change the attitudes and practices of the people with whom the work is done (Ensminger, 1957).
- **Extension Education:** It is as an applied science consisting of content derived from research, accumulated field experiences and relevant principles drawn from the behavioural sciences synthesised with useful technology into a body of philosophy, principles, content and methods focused on the problems of out of school education for adult and youth (Legans, 1969).
- **Agricultural Extension:** It is helping farmers to help themselves (Liniger, 1953).
- **Rural Extension:** It can cover an aspect or all aspects of rural development, including agricultural extension.
- **Transfer of technology**: It includes the additional functions of supplies and services. Agricultural extension is an essential and major part of technology transfer, but the terms are not synonymous. Transfer of technology is a much wider term than extension.

2.11 CHECK YOUR PROGRESS

1. Who coined the term Extension Education and when?
2. Describe briefly the growth of extension in the modern era?
3. Define and explain the term "Extension Education"?

4. State and explain three objectives of extension?
5. Describe the philosophy of extension given by Kelsey and Hearne (1967)?
6. Explain any five principles of extension?
7. "Extension education is one type of formal education". Give your reasons in support of the statement?

CHAPTER 3

Rural Development: Meaning, Definition, Concepts and Objectives

3.0 OBJECTIVES

The knowledge of the meaning, concept, definition and objectives of rural development are fundamental to rural development studies. This unit will definitely go a long way to help students' understanding of the underlying philosophy of rural development. As such, upon completion of this unit, students will be able to:

1. Define rural development
2. Analyse the concept of rural development
3. Tell the basic elements of rural development
4. List various objectives of rural development
5. Mention the approaches of rural development
6. Tell the importance of rural development
7. Find out the constraints of rural development

3.1 INTRODUCTION

The term rural development is becoming a buzz word all over the world. As most of the people on earth live in rural areas, development in true sense cannot be expected without addressing the basic necessities of this huge population. In the era of modern science and technology, a large amount of population in rural areas are still deprived of adequate nutrition, good education, proper communication, and social justice. Therefore, rural development is gaining importance in both developed and developing countries. However, until today, there is no universally accepted definition of rural development. As a concept, rural development is comprehensive and multidimensional. It means improving the quality of life of the people living in rural areas through agriculture and allied activities. As a phenomenon, rural development is the result of interactions between various physical, technological, economic, socio-cultural and institutional factors. For instance, if we want to develop a rural area through agricultural activities, there is a need to think of changing the attitude of farmers toward modern agriculture; introduction of HYV of crops, mechanization of farming, use of fertilizers, pesticides; formation of SHGs for microfinance; training of farmers for building capacities in modern agriculture; improvement of roads and communication system, provision of electricity, market etc. Therefore, it calls for a holistic approach to development. As a strategy, rural poor are always targeted in rural development. As a discipline, it has a close relationship with subjects like agriculture and allied sciences, social sciences, health sciences, engineering and management sciences.

3.2 MEANING AND DEFINITION OF RURAL DEVELOPMENT

According to the UN, rural development is a process which leads to a continuous rise in the capacity of the rural people to control their environment accompanied by a wider distribution of benefits resulting from such control.

Robert Chambers (1983) opined that rural development is a strategy to enable a specific group of people, poor rural women and men, to gain for themselves and their children more of what they want and need. It involves helping the poorest among those who seek a livelihood in the rural areas to demand and control more of the benefits of rural development. The group also includes small scale farmers, tenants and the landless.

Thus, rural development may be defined in many ways depending upon our focus and attention. However, successful rural development aims at improving the quality of life of the poor rural people through technological intervention, forming, modifying or strengthening new and old institutions and organizations for building their capacities, providing better communication facilities and implementing government policies and programmes.

3.3 ANALYSIS OF THE CONCEPT OF RURAL DEVELOPMENT

The concept of rural development can be analysed as follows:

1. It is a process of building capacities of rural people. The capacity may be build up in all aspects of life, which includes socio-economic, cultural, educational and political.
2. It ensures the increased ability of the poor rural mass to have control over their environment and resources rather than being a passive object of external control and manipulations.
3. It also ensures the participation of rural people in all developmental activities. There is an increasing concern all over the world that the poor, the needy, the unprivileged, the weaker section of the society should take an active part in the development process, so that, they can fully enjoy the benefits of development.

3.4 BASIC ELEMENTS OF DEVELOPMENT

There are at least three basic elements as given by Singh (1986), which are considered to constitute the true meaning of development. These are:

1. **Life-sustenance**: In order to survive, people have certain basic needs. These basic necessities include food, shelter and clothing. Besides, health care facilities and security are also important needs. Providing these basic necessities to all the people is of vital importance for economic growth, which is a prerequisite for development.
2. **Self-respect**: Every person and every nation seeks some basic form of self-respect, dignity and honour. Absence or denial of self-esteem indicates a lack of development initiatives.
3. **Freedom:** Freedom not only refers to political or ideological freedom but also freedom from ignorance and superstitions. A man should be free from all bondages and should live in harmony with nature.

3.5 OBJECTIVES OF RURAL DEVELOPMENT

The objectives of rural development are manifold. It manifests through the different activities taken up by different societies. However, in almost all societies, the following objectives are considered vital for the all-round development of rural people.

1. Rural people must have access to the basic life-sustaining articles, such as food, shelter and clothing. It must be made available to the rural people. Besides, there must be provision for sound health care facilities and also social security. In the absence of these, rural development can hardly be achieved.
2. The improved standard of living of poor rural people as a result of development initiatives must be reflected in increased purchasing power, better education to children, and greater attention to cultural and philanthropic activities. More job opportunities should be created for the rural people to live a better life.
3. There must be a gradual reformation of society from slavery and dependency to social and economic choice by the individual and thereby empower themselves to determine their own fate.

IGNOU (Indira Gandhi National Open University) identified the following objectives of rural development:

1. Improving the standard of living of rural people by providing food, shelter, clothing, employment and education.
2. Increasing productivity in rural areas for reducing rural poverty.
3. Ensuring peoples' participation in planning and development through decentralization of administration.
4. Ensuring distributive justice and equalization of opportunities in society.

3.6 APPROACHES OF RURAL DEVELOPMENT IN INDIA

In order to attain the objectives of rural development, as discussed earlier, different approaches need to be followed. However, there is no single, universally acceptable approach of rural development. Since development itself is a long term process; strategies are evolved to solve the rural problems. The problems of rural people are many, and approaches for their solutions also vary according to situation and magnitude. There are various schools of thought which perceive the approach of development differently and put their emphasis in a different set of factors in their theories. Let us discuss some important approaches to rural development taken up in India.

1. **Rural development projects and programmes**: Rural development projects are micro-level efforts to bring about desirable changes in rural areas. However, rural development programmes involve a large number of projects which are aligned to one another, so that; they affect various facts of rural economic and social life. Rural development programmes attempt to bring about changes in wider areas affecting a large number of people.
2. **Community development programme**: The community development programme initiated in the year 1952 made an attempt to increase the involvement of rural people in the development process. It laid emphasis on the building of infrastructure in rural areas with the active involvement of people through organizational set up of National Extension Services.
3. **Package approach**: In order to increase agricultural production per se in the country, this approach was adopted. Popularly known as package programme, the emphasis was given on the application of all improved practices, such as seeds, fertilizers, irrigation, plant protection measures and use of improved agricultural implements. The programme like Intensive Agricultural District Programme (IADP), Intensive Agricultural Area Programme (IAAP), High Yielding Varieties Programme (HYVP) are a good example of such an approach.
4. **Area approach**: In this approach, specific areas were targeted for development initiatives. The areas which need specific attention for certain problems to tackle were selected in this approach. The Drought Prone Area Programme (DPAP), Command Area Development Programme (CADP) are some of the major initiatives under this approach.
5. **Target approach**: The poor, unprivileged section of the society deprived of the benefits from the package programme, were selected under this approach. The Small Farmers Development Agency (SFDA), Marginal Farmers and Agricultural Labourers

(MFAL) were some of the programmes under this approach.

6. **Integrated rural development**: There is a fair amount of disagreement among the rural development experts in defining the concept of Integrated Rural Development. The rural economy and social structure in most of the developing countries is characterised by widespread poverty, poor health conditions, illiteracy, exploitation, inequitable distribution of land and other assets and lack of rural infrastructure and public utility. Therefore, the problem requires an approach that will take into account all these factors in devising a comprehensive strategy to foster development in rural areas.
7. **Grass root level approach or local level participation in rural development:** There is a paradigm shift of approach in rural development in recent times. The efforts are more people-centric and situation specific. It is because of the fact that the problem of the rural areas varies with the situation to situation and problems need to be solved locally using available resources. Hence, ensuring people's participation in all development efforts is becoming a prerequisite for any rural development initiative. The implications of these efforts are:
    a) Suppression of elitist elements in rural areas so that the poor people can reap the benefits of development. It was observed that the fruits of the development initiatives in the post-independence era were eaten up by the rural elites. The poor, which constitutes the larger sections of the Indian society remained untouched. As a result impact of development efforts was found to be very less. Therefore, in grass root level approach of development, the poor, the deprived class of people are given due importance.
    b) Stressing the importance of self-development rather than foreign aid;
    c) Using education as a tool to enable people to organize themselves to bring changes in society.
    d) The top-down approaches are proved to be anti-poor, and therefore, there is a great demand for a pro-poor bottom-up approach.

3.7 IMPORTANCE OF RURAL DEVELOPMENT IN INDIA

As we know that India is predominantly an agricultural based country, and the majority of the population lives in rural areas. The father of the nation rightly said that to understand the Indian mind, one must visit and study rural India. The culture, tradition, ethos and values of this ancient civilization can be seen in villages. Though the country has achieved a lot of successes in different spheres after her sixty-two years of independence, lots have to be done yet in the field of rural development. Rural India is still in the grip of poverty, illiteracy, hunger and malnourishment; lack of proper health and sanitation facility; and above all absence of scientific temperament. There is also a need to devise a programme which would empower people to decide their future course of actions by themselves to earn their livelihood. This calls for planning and implementation of various rural development policies and programmes.

At present, about 20 per cent of national GDP comes from agriculture, and 57 per cent of Indian population is employed in agriculture. There are 200 million farmers and farm workers in the country. It is also found that 2 per cent growth in agriculture can result in 8 per cent growth in other sectors. However, barring few advantageous states, in most of the states of the country are still practising the age-old farming practices. The modern method of cultivation is still a far cry in the majority of the Indian villages. The population in the country is increasing day by day, creating a lot of pressure on existing land. In order to feed this huge population, production and productivity have to be increased. Also, being a signatory of WTO agreement, India must have to put emphasis on quality products for the international market. Therefore, there is a growing need to make our farmer aware of the present demand.

There are different areas of rural development where efforts should be directed to achieve desired results. This includes the application of science and technology in agriculture and allied sectors, addressing the issues related to natural calamities, solving the problems of rural migration, utilization of rural resources, ensuring participation of rural people in all the stages of development and improvement of the socio-political conditions of the people. As suggested by FAO of the UN, the benefits of rural development should reach the needy and underprivileged sections of the society. Therefore, rural development helps to develop the self-confidence of the poor rural mass, so that they can control their environment, which is a prerequisite for the overall development of the country.

3.8 CONSTRAINT / PROBLEMS IN RURAL DEVELOPMENT

There are several problems encountered by our rural society. These problems or constraints have to be removed in order to increase the speed of rural development. Some major problems are discussed below:

1. **Poverty**: Poverty is considered to be one of the major hurdles in the path of development. Poverty refers to a level of living so low that it prevents normal development of human personality-physical, mental and social. According to Planning Commission, 21.1% people (estimated) in rural areas of our country were living Below the Poverty Line in 2007. There are different indicators of poverty, which includes roads and communication facilities, primary schools, health care facilities, fair price shops, drinking water facility, electrification; marketing facilities etc. The non-existence of any one of these indicates the extent of poverty in an area. Eradication of extreme poverty is also one of the millennium development goals of the UN.
2. **Illiteracy:** Education is the key to development. However, much has to be done to attain 100 per cent literacy. According to the 2001 census, the literacy rate in rural India is only 59.40 %. In line with the efforts of the UN, there is a need to ensure that by 2015, all children must have to receive full primary education.
3. **Small landholdings**: With the increase of population, the land, one of the major factors of production, is becoming a scarce commodity. As per National Sample Survey (2002-03), the average land holding in India was 1.06 ha only, and marginal holdings (of size 1 hectare or less) in 2002-03 constituted 70% of all operational holdings. The experts are of the opinion that the use of agricultural technology in small landholdings is very

difficult. Therefore, the need of the hour is to evolve modalities for development of appropriate technology suitable for small holdings.

4. **Malnutrition and starvation**: It is closely linked with the issue of extreme poverty as well as mass awareness. The infant mortality rate (under-1) was 54% in 2007. Moreover, in some areas of the country, due to several natural disasters, deaths out of starvation and malnutrition are still reported. Sometimes, due to lack of knowledge of a balanced diet, people suffer from various ailments.
5. **Ill-health**: Due to lack of proper health care facilities and education, people of the country are suffering from various diseases. Child mortality and a greater number of maternal death are also creating major threats to development in the country.
6. **Ignorance and lack of scientific temperament**: The issue related to lack of scientific temperament is closely associated with proper education. There is a need to make people aware of scientific phenomena behind health and sanitary problem and also to fight against all kinds of evils in society.
7. **Caste system**: Existence of the caste system also sometimes acts as a bottleneck in the process of development. The problems of the people belonging to lower caste need to be solved so as to bring them into the mainstream. Special provisions are made in the constitution of India to uplift them to a higher position.
8. **Communication and transportation**: Even after sixty-two years of independence, the communication and transport system of the country are not up to the mark. However, these two are equally important to speed up agricultural development. Though our country is marching ahead in modern information technology and communication network, many villages are yet to be connected by telephone booth and even post offices. The conditions of the rural, as well as urban roads, are also deplorable, which are very important for movement and products of goods for marketing from rural to urban areas and vice -versa.
9. **Exploitation by vested interest groups**: The very existence of

old *Jamindary* system is though not available, rural people are still in the grip of money lenders, *mahajans*, middlemen and also local level politicians. Due to poverty, lack of education and some other socio-political issues, rural people are exploited by these groups.

10. **Gender inequality**: Women are still not represented to a great extent in local as well as national decision-making bodies. Efforts are being made in this regard so that they can take an active role in the development process.

Thus, it can be concluded that much is to be done yet many things to bring rural development in true sense. The problems of the small farmers, tenants and landless labourers have to be addressed properly by implementing several programmes with a view to improving the quality of their life.

3.9 SUMMARY

In this unit, we have studied that there is no universally accepted definition of rural development. However, rural development can be defined as a process which leads to a continuous rise in the capacity of the rural people to control their environment accompanied by a wider distribution of benefits resulting from such control. The successful rural development efforts aimed at improving the quality of life of the poor rural people through technological intervention, building up of institutions and organizations for building their capacities, providing better communication facilities and implementing government policies and programmes. There are different approaches to rural development. The problems or constraints encountered by rural society have to be removed in order to increase the speed of rural development. As suggested by FAO of the UN, the benefits of rural development should reach the needy and underprivileged sections of the society.

3.10 KEYWORDS

- **Rural Development**: Rural development is a process which leads to a continuous rise in the capacity of the rural people to control their environment accompanied by a wider distribution of benefits resulting from such control.

- **Basic elements of development**: There are at least three basic elements of development, such as Life-sustenance, Self-respect and Freedom.
- **Approaches of rural development in India**: In order to attain the objectives of rural development, different approaches were being followed in India, such as rural development projects and programmes, C.D. Programme, area approach, target approach, integrated rural development approach, grass root level approach etc.

3.11 CHECK YOUR PROGRESS

1. What are the basic elements of development? Explain the concept of rural development with suitable examples.
2. "All societies must have some objectives irrespective of what development is" – Justify the statement in the light of rural development.
3. Describe 5 (five) approaches of rural development in India taken up during the post-independence period.
4. Why there is an increasing concern all over the world for local level participation in rural development?
5. What are the major constraints of development in India?
6. Why rural development is gaining importance in our country?

CHAPTER 4

Development Programmes of Pre Independence Era

4.0 OBJECTIVES

The knowledge of different development programmes of the pre-independence era is important to study the present rural development programmes. It will also help us to know the achievements and drawbacks of those programmes. This unit will definitely go a long way to help students' understanding of different development programmes of a pre-independence era. As such, upon completion of this unit, students will be able to:

- List some rural development programmes of the pre-independence era.
- List various objectives of selected programmes of the pre-independence era.
- Tell the approaches / activities of some selected programmes of the pre-independence era.
- List achievements of some selected programmes of the pre-independence era.
- Find out the limitations of some selected programmes of the pre-independence era.

4.1 INTRODUCTION

In the case of rural development, until the last quarter of the 19th century, nothing was done in India by foreign rulers. The series of famines from 1875 to 1901, numbering 18 out of 33 during the whole of the 19th century, forced the government to appoint some Commissions. They recommended rural development work. There followed by certain Acts like Land Improvement Loans Act and Agricultural Loans Act of 1888, cooperative Act of 1904 and its amendment in 1912 etc. and establishment of developments departments like Agriculture, Animal Husbandry and Veterinary and irrigation etc. But that development department could not take any comprehensive programme (Dahama and Bhatnagar, 1991) and the situation did not improve much. Considering the poor state of rural India, various attempts on rural development had also been made by different persons during the pre-independence era. Some of those programmes were Gurgaon Experiment; Servants of India Society, Poona; Sriniketon experiment; Sir Denial Hamilton's Scheme of Rural Reconstruction, Marthandam project; Gandhian Constructive programme, Adrash Sewa Sangh, Pohri; Indian Villages Service, Sarvodaya programme, Boroda experiment etc. Here, some important programmes are discussed below:

4.2 SRINIKETAN EXPERIMENT

The programme was started by R.N. Tagore in 1921 as rural development work. He believed villages as growth cones of India. He wanted decentralization, opposed science, technology, industrialisation and emphasized on spiritual aspects of life. He established Rural Reconstruction Institute at Shantiniketan in 1921. A group of eight villages was the centre of the programme. The activities of the institute were the development of agriculture, cooperatives, industries and education (Dahama and Bhatnagar, 1991).

Objectives

1. Creating an interest in people to participate in their own development.
2. Helping people to develop their own resources.
3. Developing a leader from the community to guide the people in their development process
4. Improving village sanitation.

Approach/ Activity

1. Creating a spirit of self-help
2. Developing village leadership

3. Organizing village scouts and *Brati Balika*
4. Establishing a training centre for handicrafts
5. Establishing a demonstration centre at Shantiniketan. It conducted demonstrations on farmer's holdings on improved practices, established a dairy to supply pure milk and better animals to the farmers for breeding, and established a poultry farm for the same purpose (Dahama and Bhatnagar, 1991).

Achievement

1. Successfully established health cooperatives in some villages
2. Created fund through savings in few villages
3. The marginal increase in production and income.

Reasons for Failure

1. The initial success of the project was not transferred to other villages
2. Lack of harmony between ideas and approach
3. No systematic planning
4. No market linkage
5. Lack of professional guidance to people
6. More idealistic, practical aspects were neglected.

4.3 MARTHANDAM PROJECT

The project was initiated by Dr. Spencer Hatch in 1921 at Travancore under the auspices of YMCA. The project was intended to symbolise three fold developments of spirit, mind and body. It evolved a five-sided programme-spiritual, mental, physical, economic and social. Dr. Spencer, along with the general secretary of YMCA, Mr. Paul established a demonstration centre at Marthandam. It was a central place for around 40 thickly populated, poor villages. This new movement was called Rural Reconstruction. The project covered around 40,000 populations. Marathandam was in a strategic position to serve the villages. It kept prize bulls and goat, model beehives, demonstration plot for improving grain and vegetable seeds etc. At the centre, cottage vocations were taught, and agricultural implements tested (Dahama and Bhatnagar,

1991).

Objective

The main objective of the programme was to self-help. It also tried to develop ownership feelings among the members of society. It tried to reach to the poorest of the society. Simplicity, cooperation and coordination were some other main objectives of the programme.

Approach /Activities

The demonstration centre has undertaken some activities like-

1. Establishing night school for improving literacy
2. Exhibiting reading materials and ideas about poultry, livestock etc. at the weekly market.
3. Guiding village organization
4. Initiating extension works beyond 40 villages.

Achievement

1. Success in production and selling of egg, honey etc. through egg selling and honey selling club.
2. Social activities of the centre met the mental, physical and spiritual needs of the villagers.
3. Replicate the project at Baroda.
4. Helped in establishing such centre at Mysore, Hyderabad, Egypt, Burma (now Myanmar) and Cyclone (now Sri Lanka)

Critical Review

1. Dealt with identical and stereotype activities
2. Organized in a better way than Sriniketan because of organizational strength of YMCA
3. Concentrated on income generating activities
4. Emphasised on the marketing of output which was successful
5. Provide expert advice and developed trained workers

4.4 GURGAON EXPERIMENT

The programme was started by Mr. F.L. Brayne, D.C., Gurgaon district, Punjab in 1927. It was a rural upliftment programme on a mass scale. Under this programme, a village guide was posted in each village which was to act as a channel through which the advice of experts in various departments could be passed on to the villagers (Dahama and Bhatnagar, 1991). They disseminated expert information on various aspects of agriculture, health, home improvement, female education etc. The entire district was covered by the experiment. It focused on every aspect of human life for upliftment.

Objectives

Major objectives were to convince villagers for improvement, kill fatalism by demonstration, taught better means and restrict unhealthy customs

Approach / Activity

1. Training to village guide, *patwari* on agriculture, cooperative, public health, sanitation, and veterinary.
2. Opened domestic school for women- *Grihini* School.
3. Organised health association and health centre run by trained nurses.
4. Sanitation was given top priority

Review

1. Coordinated efforts
2. Trained staff of protagonist
3. The popularization of efforts.
4. The impact was not long lasting
5. Works were done by villagers to please their district official

4.5 GANDHIAN CONSTRUCTIVE PROGRAMME – SEVAGRAM

To make villages self-sufficient and develop moral stamina to fight oppression and injustice, the Gandhian Constructive Programme was initiated. The training centre was established at Sevagram, and Mahatma Gandhi worked from there (1936). The main principles were decentralized production, equal distribution of wealth and self- sufficiency of Indian villages.

Activity/ Approach

1. Promotion of village industries
2. Promotion of basic and adult education
3. Rural sanitation
4. Upliftment of backward tribes and women.
5. Education in public health and hygiene.
6. Propagation of national language
7. Love for mother tongue
8. Economic Equality
9. The organisation of farmers, labour, students etc.

Achievements

1. It was a movement of the people, by the people and for the people.
2. Popularisation of khadi took place
3. Reduction in untouchability and caste system
4. It was a national level programme

4.6 LEARNING EXPERIENCES OF DIFFERENT DEVELOPMENT PROGRAMMES OF PRE INDEPENDENCE ERA

Though there were numbers of projects started for rural development during the pre-independence era, they had one or the other shortcomings. Though these projects were aimed at rural development and were locale-specific, yet they lacked government support and larger involvement of the people. These were around individual philosophy and gradually vanished with time. Some of the drawbacks/ limitations, as mentioned by Ray (1996) are:

1. Most of the efforts were based on individual initiatives.

2. All attempts were isolated, uneven and discontinuous.
3. Government t support and financing were not forthcoming.
4. Staffs were mostly inexperienced and untrained.
5. Involvement of the people in planning and execution, i.e. finding out the problems and their solutions were very limited
6. Association and coordination of other development departments were very limited
7. No evaluation was carried out. Hence the results were not known properly.
8. Need for proper methods and skills of approach were not realized.

4.7 SUMMARY

India had witnessed and experienced many programmes before independence for rural development in general and agriculture development in particular. Before independence, only sporadic attempts by individuals, political leaders and social workers were made in different parts of the country. Some of the significant efforts were made by Rabindranath Tagore at Shriniketan, Spencers Hatch at Marthandam, Gurgaon Experiment and Gandhian Constructive Programme at Sevagram etc. These projects were aimed at rural development and were locale specific. They lacked government support and involvement of the people. These were around individual philosophy. The common activities were the improvement of agricultural products, sanitation, education etc.

4.8 KEYWORDS

- **Sriniketan Experiment:** This programme was started by R. N. Tagore in 1921.
- **Marthandam Project:** The project was initiated by Dr. Spencer Hatch in 1921 at Travancore under the auspices of YMCA.
- **Gurgaon Experiment:** The programme was started by Mr. F.L. Brayne in 1927.
- **Gandhian Constructive Programme – Sevagram:** Initiated by M. K. Gandhi in 1936.

4.9 CHECK YOUR PROGRESS

1. Write the objectives of Sriniketan Experiment. What were the activities undertaken by this programme?
2. In which programme the village guide was posted? What were the main approaches of the programme?
3. What were the achievements of Gandhians Constructive Programme?
4. What were the salient features of Gurgaon experiment?
5. List out the shortcomings of pre-independence era's programmes.

CHAPTER 5

Development Programmes of Post Independence Era

5.0 OBJECTIVES

After completion of the unit, students will be able to

- State the objectives of Firka Development Project, Nilokheri Experiment and Etawah Pilot Project.
- Describe the approach and activities of Firka Development Project, Nilokheri Experiment and Etawah Pilot Project.
- Mention the achievements of Firka Development Project, Nilokheri Experiment and Etawah Pilot Project.

5.1 INTRODUCTION

Some more rural development programmes were organized even after independence. Three important programmes of the post-independence era are discussed below.

5.2 FIRKA DEVELOPMENT PROJECT

It was a government operated project started by erstwhile Govt. of Madras in 1946 with 34 Firkas (One Firka = 50 villages). It was initiated by Chief Minister T. Prakasam. Project collector was responsible for the programme. It aimed at the attainment of Gandhian ideal of Gram Swaraj by attacking the rural problems as a whole. It was aimed by bringing about not only educational, economic, sanitary and other improvements in villages but also by making the people self-confident. On April 1, 1950, it was extended to another 50 additional Firkas. The selection of the Firkas was based on considerations of the general backwardness of the area and the possibilities for initiating the production of handloom cloth and other cottage industries (Dahama and Bhatnagar, 1991). To associate people with the implementation of the programme, Development Committees consigning of officials and non-officials were constituted in each Firka (Ray, 1996).

Objectives

1. To develop rural communications, water supply, the formation of Panchayats, organization of cooperatives and programme for sanitation
2. To make the area self-sufficient through agricultural, irrigational and livestock improvements and development of khadi and other cottage industries.

Approach

1. To develop basic amenities like communication, water supply, sanitation.
2. To develop an institutional framework like panchayats and cooperation.
3. Attaining self-sufficiency in basic need through the development of agriculture animal husbandry, village and cottage industries.

Activities

The scheme covered areas like communication, drinking water, improved sanitation, agriculture extension, grow more food campaign, adult education and establishment of cooperatives. The scheme, which aimed at attacking the rural problems as a whole, as well as in parts, consisted of both short term and long term plans.

Achievement

- Involvement of non-governmental organization (NGOs)
- NGOs engaged in doing constructive work

Limitation

- Efforts were restricted in scope
- Lacked coordination, direct support and encouragement from

the central authority.

5.3 NILOKHERI EXPERIMENT

The experiment was started by S. K. Dey with refugees of Pakistan. It was started with 7000 refugees and later integrated with the 100 surrounding villages. Nilokhri was developed as a rehabilitation and resettlement colony for the refugees. It was built around a vocational centre. The programme is also called as "Mazdoor Manzil".

Objective

- Self-sufficiency of the community for rural- cum- urban township in all the essential requirements of life.

Approach

The philosophy of the program was to provide employment leading to help in setting livelihood, enhance confidence and ultimately better living standard. The resettlement colony acted as a growth centre. Township serves as an economical and administrative unit with all basic facilities/ services/ infrastructure.

Activities

The colony had school, an agricultural farm, poly technique training centre, dairy, poultry farm, piggery farm, horticulture garden, printing press, garment factory, engineering workshop, soap factory etc.

Achievements

- The whole experiments were very successful.
- The colony had school, agricultural farm, poly technique training centre, dairy, poultry farm, garment factory, workshop etc. to make it self sufficient.

5.4 ETAWAH PILOT PROJECT

Lt. Col. Albert Mayer of USA was the originator of the project. The project was conceived and born in 1947. It was launched by the Government of Uttar Pradesh. It was put into action with headquarter at Mahewa village (about 17 miles from Etawah, U. P.) in September 1948. It was a new experiment in rural planning, under which the task of seeking a better life and of reconstructing and rehabilitating the village was to be taken essentially by the villagers themselves (Ray, 1996). Initially the project started with 64 villages, extended to 97 and further to 125 villages. The multipurpose village level workers were introduced in the scheme. The programme is also known as "Average District Plan Programme". Low agriculture production and the poor state of farmers were the main reason for undertaking the programme.

The principles of the project were based on the principles of self-help, democracy, integrated approach, felt needs of the people, rigorous planning and realistic targets and institutional approach. It was also based on coordination and collaboration of various line department, non-government organization and input agencies. Funds were provided with both from the government of U.P. and Point-4 programme of U.S.A.

Objectives

The main objective was to see what degree of production and social improvement, initiative and co-operation could be obtained from an average area. Specifically, these were:

- to know the degree of productive and social improvement.
- to know how quickly result can be obtained.
- to know whether results remain permanent.
- to know whether it can be reproduced.

Activities

The rural problem under the project was tackled by:

a) efforts to broaden the mental horizon of the villager so that he might accept new and tested ideas which might then become self-generating and self-perpetuating, and
b) dealing with the villagers land, his tools and his surroundings.

The method of approach was educative and persuasive rather than coercive. For this, it was essential that the extension workers live in the villages, prove themselves to be friends of the villagers and win their confidence. The pilot programme included the introduction of improved agricultural and animal husbandry practices, public health education, literacy campaigns, improvement of cottage industries, training in repairing and evolving simple agricultural implements.

Achievement

Agriculture development was the most significant achievement-

- Improved wheat crop production
- The area under vegetable was extended
- Multipurpose concept of village level worker was introduced.
- Acted as a common platform for nation building departments.
- Introduced improved agricultural and animal husbandry practices, public health education, literacy campaigns and improvement of college industries.
- The pioneering work of the project had in large measure was responsible for the scheme of community projects which figured so prominently in India's First Five Year Plan and formed a vital part of the Second Five Year Plan.

5.5 SUMMARY

India witnessed and experienced three important programmes after independence for rural development in general and agriculture development in particular. These were the Firka Development Project, Nilokheri Experiment and Etawah Pilot Project. All the programmes were sponsored by the Government. All the programmes achieved some success.

5.6 KEYWORDS

- **Firka Development Project:** It was a government operated project started by Govt. of Madras in 1946.
- **Nilokheri Experiment:** The experiment was started by S. K. Dey at Nilokheri with refugees of Pakistan. It was started with 7000 refugees and later integrated with the 100 surrounding villages.
- **Etawah Pilot Project:** The project worked out with the

assistance of Mr. Albert Mayer was launched by Government of Uttar Pradesh in Etawah in 1948.

- **Multipurpose Village Level Worker:** It was introduced in Etawah Pilot Project.

5.7 CHECK YOUR PROGRESS

1. What are the main objectives of Nilokheri Experiment?
2. In which project, the concept of Multipurpose Village Level Worker, was introduced? Write the achievements of the project.
3. What was the popular name of Nilokheri Experiment? What were the main activities of Nilokheri Experiment?

CHAPTER 6

Community Development Programme

6.0 OBJECTIVES

This chapter aims to help the students understanding about India's Community Development Programme and National Extension Service. The unit will enable the students to comprehend definitions, objectives, philosophy and principles of Community Development Programme. It will also help the students to differentiate extension education from Community Development Programme. After completion of the unit, students will be able to:

- Describe the concepts, meaning and definition of the Community Development Programme
- Mention the objectives of the Community Development Programme in India
- State the principles of Community Development
- Describe the philosophy behind community development programme
- List the faiths behind community development
- Describe the organisational structure of the Community Development Programme in India
- Analyse India's Community Development Programme
- Describe the National Extension Service (NES) of India.
- List the major elements involved in India's Community Development and extension process
- Compare NES with CDP
- Find out the similarities and dissimilarities between C.D. and Extension Education

6.1 INTRODUCTION

The Grow More Food Campaign (GMFC) was India's first organised effort to increase food production. It was launched in 1943. After independence, due attention has been given for the development of the public extension system in India. The GMFC was evaluated in 1952 by a government-appointed committee. One of the recommendations of the committee was that an extension agency should be set up for rural work which would reach every farmer and assist in the coordinated development of rural life. It was out of this background and experience that India's Community Development Programme (CDP) was initiated in 2nd October 1952. The central objective of the CDP was to secure the total development of the material and human resources of rural areas.

6.2 CONCEPTS, MEANING AND DEFINITION

Community development is used to include any and every effort towards the advance of community interest. Community development is a compound as well as an exclusive term. Its two components are a) Community and b) Development.

A. The Community

A community is a group of people, who live in a geographical area and have an interest in each other for the purpose of making a living. It is a form of a social organization existing between the family and state. A community, while in itself consists of several parts, is also a part of a larger social system. Some of the important characteristics of the community are (1) Communities are close-knit entities (2) Their customs are interrelated (3) These communities are complexes of sub-group relationship and (4) There is a distinguished leadership within the community (Dahama and Bhatnagar, 1991).

B. Development

The term development means growth or maturation. It is a positive change. It implies gradual and sequential phases of change (Dahama and Bhatnagar, 1991).

The term Community Development originated from Cambridge in

England. In 1948, the Cambridge Summer Conference on African Administration recommended this term defining it as a movement designed to promote better living for the whole community with the active participation, if possible on the initiative of the community, but if this initiative is not forthcoming spontaneously, by the use of techniques for arousing and stimulating it in order to secure its active and enthusiastic response to the movement (Ray, 1996).

According to United Nations (1956), community development is a process by which the efforts of the people themselves are united with those of the governmental authorities to improve the economic, social and cultural conditions of the communities, to integrate these communities into the life of the nation and to enable them to contribute fully to national progress.

The International Cooperation Administration (1957) stated that community development is a process of social action in which the people of a community organize themselves for planning and action, define their common and individual needs and problems, make group and individual plans to meet their needs and solve their problems, execute these plans with a maximum of reliance upon community resources, and supplement these resources when necessary, with services and materials from governmental and non-governmental agencies outside the community.

Community development is a method by which people who live in local villages or communities are involved in helping to improve their own economic and social conditions and thereby become effective working groups in programmes of national development. It assumed that people become dynamic if they permitted to make own decisions and helped to carry on the programme (Taylor *et al.* 1956).

Mukherji (1967), summarised these concepts by stating that Community Development is a process of change from the traditional way of living in rural communities to progressive ways of living. It is a method by which people can be assisted to develop themselves on their own capacity and resources; It is a programme for accomplishing certain activities in the field concerning the welfare of the rural people. It is also a movement for progress with certain ideological content.

6.3 OBJECTIVES OF COMMUNITY DEVELOPMENT PROGRAMME IN INDIA

The Ministry of Community Development and Cooperation, Govt. of India (1962) stated the Specific objectives of the community development programme as follows:

1. To assist each village in having effective panchayats, cooperatives and schools; and
2. through these village institutions plan and carry out integrated, multiphased family, village, block and district plans for:
   a) increasing agricultural production
   b) improving existing village crafts and industries and organizing new ones
   c) providing minimum essential health services and improving health practices
   d) providing required educational facilities for children and an adult education programme
   e) providing recreational facilities and programmes
   f) improving housing and family living conditions, and
   g) providing programmes for village women and youth.

According to Dahama and Bhatnagar (1991), the objectives behind the Community Development Programme in India was to develop the resources of the people numbering about 640 million who from the rural population (at that time).

6.4 PRINCIPLES OF COMMUNITY DEVELOPMENT

According to the United Nations Economic and Social Council, the guiding principles of community development are summarized as follows (Ray, 1996):

1. Activities undertaken must correspond to the basic needs of the community; the first project should be initiated in response to the expressed needs of the people.
2. Full and balanced community development requires concerted action and the establishment of multipurpose programmes
3. Changed attitudes in people are as important as the material achievements of community projects during the initial stages of development.

4. Community development aims at increased and better participation of the people in community affairs, revitalization of existing forms of local government and transition towards effective local administration where it is not yet functioning.
5. The identification, encouragement and training of local leadership should be a basic objective in any programme.
6. Greater reliance on the participation of women and youth in community projects invigorates development programmes, establishes them on a wide basis and secures long-range expansion.
7. To be fully effective, self-help projects for communities require both intensive and extensive assistance from the government.
8. Implementation of community development programme on a national scale requires the adoption of consistent policies, specific administrative arrangement, recruitment and training of personnel, mobilization of local and national resources and organization of research, experimentation and evaluation.
9. The resources of voluntary and non-governmental organizations should be fully utilized in community development programmes at the local, national and international levels.
10. Economic and social progress at the local level necessitates parallel development on a wider national scale.

6.5 PHILOSOPHY BEHIND COMMUNITY DEVELOPMENT PROGRAMME

According to Dahama and Bhatnagar (1991) philosophies on which the community development programme should be based are as follows:

1. **Work-based on "felt needs":** The programme should help the community to solve some of the problems which it feels are existent.
2. **Work-based on the assumption that people want to be free from poverty and pain:** It is assumed that the members of the community want a standard of living that allows them to be free from pain caused by lack of sufficient food, lack of sanitary conditions lack clothing and shelter. On the social side, it assumed that people have four basic wishes:

a) security,
b) recognition,
c) response, and
d) new experience.

3. It is assumed that people wish to have freedom in controlling their owns lines and deciding the forms of economic, religious, educational and political institutions, under which they will live.
4. **People's values given due consideration:** It is presumed that cooperation, group decision-making, self-initiative, social responsibility, leadership, trustworthiness and ability to work are included in the programme.
5. **Self-help:** The people actually plan and work on the solution of their problems themselves. If the problems of the community are entirely ameliorated through the efforts of some outside agency, then the development of such things as group decision-making, self-initiative, self–reliance, leadership, etc., will not be forthcoming and it cannot be said that the community is developing.
6. **People are the greatest resource:** It is by getting the participation of the people in improvement activities that they become developed
7. The programme involves a change in attitudes, habits, ways of thinking, relationships among people in the level of knowledge and intellectual advancement of people, change in their skills, i.e., practices of agriculture, health, etc.

6.6 FAITHS BEHIND COMMUNITY DEVELOPMENT

Dahama and Bhatnagar (1991) also mentioned some faiths behind community development. These are:

1. Community Development has based on the faith that rural people have the capacity to improve if helped.
2. People's participation is significant. The programme should fully involve them in the process of improving themselves through their own efforts.
3. It has to be organized on a small community-unit basis.

This gives the advantage of mutual helpfulness, intimate relationships and mutual confidence.

4. It has faith in the democratic approach.
5. It has faith in science and technology.
6. It has faith in social justice.

6.7 COMMUNITY DEVELOPMENT PROGRAMME (CDP) IN INDIA

The success of Etawah Pilot Project encouraged Indian planners to take a similar programme throughout India. CDP conceptualized to transform social and economic aspects of village community irrespective of caste, religion, ethnicity or economic status. The programme was launched in India on 2nd October 1952 with 55 Community Development Projects.

Organisational Structure

Each project had an operational area of about 400 to 500 square miles, comprising 300 villages and a population of about 2 lakhs. Each project area was divided into 3 development blocks, each consisting of about 100 villages with a population of 60 to 70 thousand. The project was headed by a Project Officer, and a number of subject matter Extension Officers in the disciplines of agriculture, animal husbandry, cooperation, industries, rural engineering, social education etc. Each project had about 60 multi-purpose Village Level Workers (VLWs). One VLW looks after 5 to 10 villages, and each block had 20 VLWs. They were government appointed extension functionary at the lowest level. Their activities were multipurpose in nature. The multipurpose VLWs were common to the departments engaged in rural development work.

Creation of Block Administration as a team had been a unique feature for administering development programmes in rural India. Conceptually and functionally it was quite different from the other established Government offices. A block office had a Block Development Officer (BDO) as the head, and a number of Extension Officers in Agriculture, Animal Husbandry, Cooperation, Industries, Rural Engineering and Social Education etc. It had also 20 multipurpose Village Level Workers. The extension officers were under the technical control of the respective district level officers for technical programme implementation and administratively under the control of BDO.

The whole block staff, including the VLWs, constituted a development team with BDO as the leader. The BDO is to be an entrepreneur of development in the block and not an administrator. The BDO has no responsibility for law and order or revenue administration. The job is to get coordinated teamwork among the staff and to educate all members of the staff and as many village groups and village leaders as possible on the whole development programme and process. BDO is the key man in the whole community development programme.

6.8 CRITICAL ANALYSIS OF INDIA'S COMMUNITY DEVELOPMENT PROGRAMME

Taylor and others (1965), made a critical analysis of India's Community Development Programme. Some of their observations are as follows.

1. Government personnel in India have not only assumed major responsibility for determining what the needs of the villagers were, but assumed the responsibility for prescribing how these needs could and should be met.
2. As a corollary to this, village leaders had difficulty in mobilizing their people to undertake projects which they themselves had not selected.
3. Little, if any, use was made of the process of helping villagers to analyzes their most commonly felt needs and to organize for self-help improvement undertakings. There was an absence of understanding the basic purpose of generating local group dynamics.
4. The Village Level Workers felt they were best prepared to render assistance in the field of agriculture and least prepared to stimulate group action. They said they were not very successful in mobilizing or catalyzing local village groups because they had not received much training in this field.
5. The Village Level Workers were compelled to give much time to record keeping and submission of reports, which sharply

reduced the time they could give to extension and community development work.

6. The Social Education Organizers whose role was originally described as being specialists in community organization very often appeared to have no clear-cut concept of their roles and quite often said their chief accomplishments were organizing and staging social or cultural programmes.
7. The Block Specialists in the field of Cooperation were enthusiastic and indicated that they were promoting a great deal of propaganda, but were able to report a few concrete results of their efforts.

They gave some reasons for the failure of India's Community Development Programme. These were:

1. The programme was validly conceived, but because of its magnitude, it has been difficult to recruit and train enough persons to play all the essential roles, to adequately staff the many local areas where the programme was in operation.
2. It has proved to be not only impossible but not feasible, to attempt to compensate for these inevitable weaknesses by administrative direction from above: and
3. The only remedy for these weaknesses is to reorient the programme and begin strengthening its grassroots foundation component, work at the village level.

6.9 NATIONAL EXTENSION SERVICE (NES)

The people in all the project areas of CDP responded enthusiastically, and the need for a rapid expansion of the programme to other parts of the country was urgently felt. Limited resources, however, did not permit a rapid expansion of the CD Projects. A year later, in 1953, the National Extension Service (NES) programme was launched with the idea of having wider coverage at less cost and more people's participation.

Organisational Structure of NES

Each NES block had about 100 villages and about 65 thousand population. The NES block was headed by a Block Development Officer (BDO) and had a number of Extension Officers (Eos). For the NES blocks, funds were drastically reduced, and the number of multipurpose VLWs was brought down to 10. Roles of BDOs, EOs and VLWs were same with CDP. NES was thought of as the agency and CD as the method to bring about socio-economic transformation of the rural people.

It was a major development in the sphere of rural reconstruction in India. Since the basic idea underlying both the CD and NES programmes was the same, the two were integrated under one agency at the Centre as well as in the States. Both the programmes were complementary and interwoven and ran concurrently. NES was viewed as the permanent setup for extension in the country, and it was intended to cover the entire country with an organization for agriculture and rural development within a period of about 10 years.

The momentum gained by the NES programme was intensified by converting some selected NES blocks to Community Development Blocks (CDB). The programme was initiated in 1954. The NES blocks which produced good results and where people's participation had been in abundance, were selected for the purpose. In these blocks, funds were increased, and some additional staff was provided.

6.10 MAJOR ELEMENTS INVOLVED IN INDIA'S COMMUNITY DEVELOPMENT AND EXTENSION PROCESS

According to Dahama and Bhatnagar (1991), the major elements constituting the foundation of the N.E.S. and Community Development Programme in India are:

1. **The objective:** i.e. to raise the economic and social level of villagers of India.
2. **General elements requiring change:** Farm, home, public services and the village community.
3. **Specific elements requiring change:** Crops, livestock, living conditions, services like health, education, cooperatives, organization, developing leadership etc.
4. **Elements that need change:** The people, i.e. men, women and youth living in villages.

5. **Change agents:**
   a) Voluntary local leaders,
   b) *Professional:* Village Level Workers and extension specialists.
6. **Professional and material resources:** The staff of Blocks, District, State and National levels with their resources, now engaged in the programme

6.11 COMPARISON OF NES WITH CDP

1. NES emphasized to cover large areas at less cost and more peoples participation. But in case of CDP fund was more.
2. In CDP, there were Community Development Project where three blocks were there. But in the case of NES, there were only NES blocks, projects.
3. Numbers of VLWs were reduced to 10 in NES. In CDP, there were 20 VLWs per block at the village level.
4. Some NES blocks were converted to CD blocks based on performance and where people's participation was more. In such blocks, funds were increased, and some additional staffs were provided
5. The basic idea underlying both the CD and NES programmes was the same; the two were integrated under one agency at the Centre as well as in the States.
6. Both the programmes were complementary and interwoven and ran concurrently.
7. NES was viewed as the permanent setup for extension in the country, and it was intended to cover the entire country with an organization for agriculture and rural development within a period of about 10 years.

6.12 SIMILARITIES AND DISSIMILARITIES BETWEEN C.D. AND EXTENSION EDUCATION

Cornell University of the United States of America studied the differences between extension education and community development, as revealed by the various statements of objectives, processes, forms and principles. Rudramurthy (1964) reported some information about the study, which is given below:

Similarities in Relation to Objectives

1. To improve social and economic development
2. Tackles the problem at the people's level.
3. Basically an educational approach
4. Recognizes that people need help if they are to help themselves.
5. Designed to extend knowledge to rural people
6. Aimed at bringing about change.

Similarities in Relation to Form

1. A government-sponsored and supported organization.
2. An organization emphasizing cooperation
3. Permits great flexibility in types of organization to do the job.

Similarities in Relation to Process

1. Both are an educational process.
2. Both are democratic processes
3. Both are involvement processes- involvement of rural people.
4. Extension education and community development are educational, democratic, involvement processes.

Dissimilarities in Relation to Objectives

Extension Education	Community Development
1. Emphasis on the individual. 2. Education aimed at individual development obtains economic and social improvement. 3. Have as its main theme the individual's needs. 4. Emphasises decision-making for change by individuals and families.	1. Emphasis on cooperation 2. Education aimed at groups of individuals to work collectively to obtain economic and social improvement. 3. Has as its main theme the community's needs 4. Emphasises decision-making by groups and representatives of groups.

Dissimilarities in Relation to Form

Sr. No.	Extension Education	Community Development
1.	The extension is an educational arm of Government, usually through educational institutions or other Government departments.	Community Development is usually a direct Government approach to the straight line organization
2.	Emphasizes an organization that either carries out educational services directly or transmits knowledge from other resources to people.	Emphasises the coordination of service agencies by a working team made up of representatives of different services
3.	Usually represents a transfer of responsibility from administering Government organization to another "Educational Group".	Usually, a tight control held by a government administering agency to cut across the participation of governmental departments: (a) To recognize and include the various departments that must provide service (b) To eliminate departmental reluctance to participate.
4.	Permits cooperation between departments and agencies.	Forces departments and agencies to participate
5.	Essentially a "Branch" of the Department of Agriculture.	Essentially a branch of government serving several departments of the government.
6.	Not directly involved in the promotion of local Units of the government.	Tied into the promotion of local units of the government.

6.13 SUMMARY

Community Development is a process of change from the traditional way of living of rural communities to progressive ways of living, as a method by which people can be assisted to develop themselves on their own capacity and resources, as a programme for accomplishing certain activities in field concerning the welfare of the rural people, and as a movement for progress with a certain ideological content. India's community Development Programme was started on 2nd October 1952. The objective behind the Community Development Programme in India is to develop the resources of the rural population. CDP had numbers of principle and philosophies. Though the programme was implemented in the whole country, it was not successful in all cases. NES was implemented in parallel to the CDP with less fund and staffs. The basic idea underlying both the CD and NES programmes was the same; the two were integrated under one agency at the Centre as well as in the States.

6.14 KEYWORDS

- **Community Development:** Community Development is a process of change from the traditional way of living of rural communities to progressive ways of living, as a method by which people can be assisted to develop themselves on their own capacity and resources, as a programme for accomplishing certain activities in field concerning the welfare of the rural people, and as a movement for progress with a certain ideological content.
- **Community Development Programme:** It was launched on 2nd October 1952. The central objective of the CDP was to secure the total development of the material and human resources of rural areas and to develop local leadership and self- governing institutions.
- **National Extension Service:** National Extension Service (NES) programme was launched in 1953 with an idea of having wider coverage at less cost and more people's participation in comparison to CDP

6.15 CHECK YOUR PROGRESS

1. What do you mean by the term Community Development?
2. What are the principles of India's Community Development Programme?
3. Mention the objectives of the Community Development Programme in India.
4. Describe the philosophy behind community development programme.
5. What is the organisational structure of the Community Development Programme in India?
6. What are the weaknesses of India's Community Development

Programme?

7. Describe briefly the National Extension Service (NES) of India.
8. What are the elements involved in India's Community Development?
9. Find out the dissimilarities between C.D. and Extension Education?

CHAPTER 7

Panchayati Raj System

7.0 OBJECTIVES

This chapter aims to help the students understand the Panchayati Raj System of India. The unit will enable the students to understand the three tires system of Panchayati Raj and their functions. After completion of the unit, students will be able to:

- Describe the concept of Democratic Decentralisation
- List some important features of the 73rd Constitutional Amendment Act, 1992
- Mention the organizational structures of the Panchayati Raj system
- Describe the standing committees of Gaon Panchayat, Panchayat Samiti and Zila Parishad
- State the power and functions of Gram Panchayat
- State the power and functions of Panchayat Samiti
- State the power and functions of Zilla Parishad
- Mention the sources of income for Panchayats
- Describe Gram Sabha and its functions.

7.1 INTRODUCTION

Rural development had engaged the attention of the Indian leadership even before Independence. The goals of development in general and rural development, in particular, have been placed in the Constitution and the Five Year Plans. The Constitution has laid down the goal in terms of building a socialist, secular and democratic society. In order to realise these goals, it becomes necessary to devise institutional mechanisms, mobilize resources (both human and material), and transform existing institutional structures and value patterns with a view to building a new social and economic order based on the values of equality, freedom and justice. Changing the existing institutional structures and social relationships is not an easy task. Thus, it became necessary to simultaneously initiate two processes- one for reorienting and, if necessary, even restructuring existing institutional structure and secondly, of building new institutional structures which could provide a base for the accomplishment of new goals.

The philosophy of development that emerged in India after Independence emphasized the involvement of the people into a structure that would enable them to actively participate in the process of decision-making. In order to bring democracy to the grassroots level and involve people in decision-making, an experiment was done with the devolution of power to the elected representatives and allocation of responsibility and financial resources as it was felt that this would be a major institutional device for the development of rural areas.

7.2 DEMOCRATIC DECENTRALISATION AND PANCHAYATI RAJ

In order to evaluate the working of Community Development Programme and to suggest ways and means overcome the shortfalls of the programme, the Study Team on Community Projects and National Extension Service with Balvantray Mehta as Chairman was appointed by the Committee on Plan Projects of the Planning Commission in 1957. The committee observed that one of the least successful aspects of CD and NES work is its attempt to evoke popular initiative and recommended Democratic Decentralisation.

The word 'Democracy' is derived from the Greek word 'demos' meaning the people and *Kratos* meaning authority. i.e. in a democracy, all authority originates from the people. Decentralisation means the distribution of functions and powers from a central authority to regional and local authorities. Democratic Decentralization means that the government which has derived its authority from the people redistributes it to some extent to the people for decision and action at the local level. This is popularly known as Panchayat Raj in India (Ray, 1996). The policy of Democratic Decentralization envisages-

1. the establishment of elected and organically linked democratic bodies at the village, block and district level;
2. the entrustment of all planning and developmental activities to these bodies; and
3. transfer of adequate resources to these bodies to enable them to discharge duties.

Panchayati Raj system came into existence in 1959 with the twin objectives of democratic decentralization and local participation in plan programmes. The states of Rajasthan and Andhra Pradesh became the pioneers. The other states followed, and by the end of a decade, Panchayati Raja had been established in different states of the country. It was hailed as a revolutionary and historic step in the context of development.

The Balvantray Mehta report recommended a three-tier system of *Panchayati Raj* Institutes (PRI) with the village *Panchayat* at the lowest level, a *Zilla Parishad* at the apex (district level), and a *Panchayat Samiti* at the intermediate (block level).

Asoka Mehta Committee (1977) again evaluated the Panchayati Raj Institute (PRI). They abolished three tire system of PRI and introduced two tires by abolishing middle tire, i.e. Panchayat Samiti. During the decade of 1990, it was realised that without constitutional power, the self-government couldn't be fruitful; therefore the Central Government passed the 73rd Constitutional Amendment Act in 1992, which became effective from 20th April 1993 (from the date of publication in the Gazette of India). The Act again introduced three tire system of PRI.

7.3 SOME IMPORTANT FEATURES OF 73RD CONSTITUTIONAL AMENDMENT ACT, 1992

Constitutional Status: The 73rd Constitutional Amendment Act was passed in 1992 but became effective from 20th April 1993 after being published in the Gazette of India. This was included as Part IX of the Constitution of India. The rights and duties of the Panchayats have been included in Schedule XI of the Constitution.

Three Leveled Systems: The Legislature of a state may, by law, make provisions for three levelled system of panchayat at the village level, intermediate level and district level.

Election: The representatives are elected for 5 years by the electorate of a Panchayat area.

Reservation of Seats: Some seats in the Panchayat shall be reserved for the Scheduled Castes, Scheduled Tribes and Women. The number of reserved seats for Scheduled Castes and Scheduled Tribes will be proportionate to the ratio of the population of SCs and STs to Total Population of the Panchayat area. One-third of the total seat will be reserved for women. It will include the reserved seats for SCs and STs.

Responsibility: Panchayats have two main responsibilities:

1. To plan for economic development and social justice.
2. To implement these plans.

Powers and Authorities: According to the Constitution, Panchayats shall be given powers and authority to function as institutions of self-government. The following powers and responsibilities are to be delegated to Panchayats at the appropriate level:

1. Preparation of Plan for economic development and social justice.
2. Implementation of schemes for economic development and social justice in relation to 29 subjects given in Eleventh Schedule of the Constitution
3. To levy, collect and appropriate taxes, duties, tolls and fees.

It may also provide the Panchayat for making grants-in-aid to form the Consolidated Fund of the State. These funds can be used for implementing the plans.

Constitution of Finance Commission: Finance Commission has to be constituted in every state to review the financial position of the Panchayats and to make a recommendation to the Governor regarding the allocation of fund to be Panchayats.

7.4 ORGANIZATIONAL STRUCTURE OF PANCHAYATI RAJ SYSTEM

A. Organisational Structure of Gaon Panchayat

This is at the lowest level. It consists of

a) One president – directly elected by people.
b) One vice president – to be elected from among the members of Gaon Panchayat.
c) Ten members – directly elected by people.

The Office of the president is of great importance. He is charged with the responsibility of supervision and coordination of the activities of the Panchayat. He is an ex-officio member of the Panchayati Samiti and participates in its decision-making as well as in the election of the *Pradhan* and of the members of various Standing Committees. He acts as the executive head of the Panchayat, represents it in the Panchayat Samiti as its spokesman and coordinates its activities and those of other local institutions like cooperatives. The Panchayat secretary and the village Level Worker are the two officers at the Panchayat level to assist the President in administration.

As the funds of the *Panchayats* are meagre, the *Panchayat* Secretary is usually appointed by the *Panchayat,* on a part-time basis. He mainly assists the *Panchayats* in recording decisions, Keeping minutes, preparing budget estimates and reports, and does other sundry jobs like preparing notices, explaining circulars, or legal provisions, helping in organising *Gram Sabha* meetings etc.

B. Organizational Structure of Panchayat Samiti

This is at the middle level. It consists of:

a) One president – to be elected by the elected members of the Panchayat Samiti.
b) One vice president - to be elected by the elected members of the Panchayat Samiti.
c) Members:
   i) One member from each Gaon Panchayat area to be directly elected by people.

ii) President of the Gaon Panchayats falling within the jurisdiction of the Panchayat Samiti.

iii) Members of Parliament and Legislative Assembly.

As the Chief Executive Officer of the *Panchayat Samiti*, the Block Development Officer is responsible for implementing the resolutions of the *Samiti* and its Standing Committees. He prepares the budget of the *Samiti* and places it before the *Samiti* for approval. He prepares the annual report of the *Samiti* and sends it to the *Zilla Parishad* and the State Government. He receives policy guidance from the *Panchayat Samiti* and is responsible to the President of the *Samiti* for his actions.

C. Organizational Structure of Zilla Parishad

It is at the top level. It consists of:

a) One president – elected from among the directly elected members of Zilla Parishad.

b) One vice president - elected from among the directly elected members of Zilla Parishad.

c) Members:

   i) Members directly elected from the Zilla Parishad constituencies of the district,

   ii) Presidents of the Panchayat Samiti.

   iii) Members of House of People and Member of Legislative Assembly.

7.5 STANDING COMMITTEES OF GAON PANCHAYAT

There are three standing committees of Gaon Panchayat; they are:

a) Development committee.

b) Social justice committee and

c) Social welfare committee.

Members: Each committee shall consist of not less than three or more than four members elected from among the elected members of the Gaon Panchayats.

Functions: The standing committee shall perform the functions relating to the development of the rural areas and its people to the extent powers are delegated from the Gaon Panchayat.

7.6 STANDING COMMITTEES OF PANCHAYAT SAMITI

There are three standing committees of Panchayat Samiti. These are general standing committee; finance, audit and planning committee and social justice committee.

Members: Each standing committee shall consist of such number of members not exceeding six including the Chairman, as may be specified by the Panchayat Samiti and chosen by the Panchayat Samiti from amongst its members.

Functions: The standing committee shall perform the functions relating to the development of the rural areas and its people to the extent powers are delegated from the Anchalik Panchayat.

7.7 STANDING COMMITTEES OF ZILLA PARISHAD

There are four standing committees of Zila Parishad. These are general standing committee, finance and audit committee, social justice committee and planning and development committee.

Members: Each standing committee shall consist of such number of members not exceeding five, including the Chairman as specified by the Zilla Parishad from amongst its members whose terms will be one year at a time.

Functions: Standing committees shall perform functions to the extent; powers are delegated to them by the Zilla Parishad.

7.8 POWER AND FUNCTIONS OF GRAM PANCHAYAT

Gaon Panchayats have two-fold functions-civic and developmental. Civic functions include sanitation, water supply, construction and maintenance of roads, lighting, maintenance of burial grounds, primary education etc. In addition, the Panchayat also acts as the agent of the Panchayat Samiti in executing schemes of development at the village level. Powers are vested to Gram Panchayat to perform various functions. Some important functions are mentioned below.

1. Prepare an annual plan and annual budget for Gram Panchayat area, organising relief operation during natural calamities, removing encroachment from public places, organizing voluntary services and collecting donations for public works

and maintaining vital statistics of the villages.

2. Identification and implementation of programmes of below Rs. 50,000/- in collaboration with agriculture cooperation, irrigation and allied departments. Development of wasteland, grazing land etc.
3. Improvement of the local breed of live stocks, development of fodder land etc.
4. Development of village's fisheries.
5. Planting of roadside trees, social forestry etc.
6. Organising awareness camp, exhibition, training programmes etc. on agriculture, Khadi and village industries etc. and works for their development.
7. Construction of rural housing and allotment of land for constructing a residential house
8. Protecting drinking water scheme/plant.
9. Construction of the rural road drains etc.
10. Rural electrification including a selection of a site for electrification, providing and maintenance of lighting system at public places.
11. Increasing source for non-conventional energy, including improved chullah maintenance of implements of non-conventional energy source installed at rural areas.
12. Increasing awareness and participation of rural peoples for income generating and poverty eradication programmes, selection of beneficiaries for such programme.
13. Increasing awareness and participation of rural people for primary and middle school education. Confirming the attendance of teachers and students for such school
14. Implementing an adult education programme and non-formal education
15. Establishing rural library
16. Propagating social and cultural activities.
17. Controlling cattle-buffalo market
18. Maintaining village sanitation.
19. Implementing family welfare programme, preventive and control measures against epidemics.

20. Involvement in women and child development programmes.
21. Participating in a welfare programme for physically and mentally handicap persons.
22. Any other functions as instructed by Panchayat and Rural Development Department

7.9 POWER AND FUNCTIONS OF PANCHAYAT SAMITI

The Panchayat Samitis are entrusted with developmental functions. They have executive responsibilities in the matter of primary education, health, sanitation and communication. They also supervise the work of Village Panchayat. The Panchayat Samiti is the most powerful body entrusted with developmental functions like planning for increased agricultural production, animal husbandry, and village industries; improvement and construction of irrigation wells, promotion of cooperatives, provision of hostels for Scheduled Castes/Scheduled Tribes/Backward Classes, planting of trees, input supplies and their distribution, women and child welfare, family planning etc. Powers are given to Panchayat Samiti to carry out the different functions out of which some are listed below.

1. Preparing an annual plan for its activities and submitted to Zila Parishad for incorporating in its district plan. Compilation of annual plans of Gram Panchayats under its jurisdiction and sending to Zila Parishad, preparation of annual budget of Panchayat Samitee and sending to Zila Parishad for its approval.
2. Helping in relief operations during natural calamities.
3. Identification and implementation of different agricultural schemes (between Rs. 50,000/ to Rs.1,00,000/-) in collaboration with agriculture, co-operation, irrigation and allied departments, storage and distribution of pesticides, farmer's training etc.
4. Helping governments and Zila Parishad for their land development and land conservation programmes.
5. Assisting Governments and Zila Parishad to construct and protecting minor irrigation projects, to implement watershed development programmes etc.
6. Planning for implementing poverty eradication programmes.

7. Protecting veterinary services, preventing epidemics against livestock.
8. Expanding fisheries.
9. Development of village and cottage industries
10. Implementation of house building programmes and distribution of land for a residential house.
11. Construction and maintenance of rural water supply schemes.
12. Tree plantation at the roadside and other social forestry.
13. Expansion of non-conventional energy source
14. Development of primary and middle school building etc.
15. Organizing training for village craftsman etc.
16. Development of social and cultural programmes etc.
17. Encouraging voluntary organization to involve women and child development programmes.
18. Implementing programmes for physically and mentally retarded peoples.
19. Expanding the programmes for the welfare of SC, ST, OBC and other weaker section.
20. Expanding rural electrification.

7.10 POWER AND FUNCTIONS OF ZILLA PARISHAD

It should be the function of a Zilla Parishad to prepare plans for economic development and social justice of the district and ensure the coordinated implementation of such plan. The Zila Parishad exercise general supervision over the working of the Panchayat Samities and advises the government on the implementation of the developmental schemes. They have some specific executive function in the establishment, maintenance and expansion of the secondary, vocational and industrial school. Zilla Parishad is mainly entrusted with coordinating and planning functions along with a few executive functions. Some of the important functions of Zilla Parishad are examination and approval of the budgets of Panchayat Samitis, distribution of funds between the various Block, coordination and consolidation of Block plans of the activities of Panchayat Samitis. Some important functions of Zila Parishad are:

1. Implementing agriculture-related programmes for their

development.
2. Implementing various schemes for development of irrigation, groundwater and watershed.
3. Development of horticulture
4. Maintaining of the statistic of panchayats, their activities etc.
5. Implementing and maintenance of rural electrification schemes
6. Programme for soil conservation
7. Development of regulated market
8. Gradation of agricultural products and quality maintenance.
9. Social forestry
10. Animal husbandry and dairy farm development
11. Development of minor forest products, energy and fodder
12. Development of fisheries
13. Development of small, cottage and food processing industries
14. Development and maintenance of rural road
15. Development and maintenance of hospital etc.
16. Construction of the rural house
17. Promotion of primary and middle school education
18. The welfare of the weaver section
19. Implementing a poverty eradication programme
20. Promotion of small savings

7.11 SOURCES OF INCOME FOR PANCHAYAT

The main sources of income of panchayat are:

- Share in land revenue
- Revenue earned from the settlement of hatt, fisheries, etc
- House taxes & other taxes
- Fees for providing amenities, cess and tolls
- Contribution and grants.
- Fine and penalties etc.

Rural people have got a noble duty to ensure that the Panchayati Raj bodies can mobilize resources from the above sources so that these bodies can work for the socio-economic development of the areas.

7.12 GRAM SABHA

"Gram Sabha" means a body consisting of persons registered in the electoral rolls relating to a village comprised within the area of "Gram Panchayat".

The Gram Sabha has been designed to be the place where villagers will discuss development issues, plan accordingly, initiate development programmes and select beneficiaries for the schemes. All the illegible voters of the village are the members of the Gram Sabha. Generally, the meeting of Gram Sabha is held at an interval of three months.

Functions of Gram Sabha (under Assam Panchayat Act, 1994): Gram Sabha shall consider the following matters and may make recommendations and suggestions to the Gaon Panchayats;

- To report in respect of the development programme of the Gaon Panchayat relating to the preceding year and development programme proposed to be undertaken during the current year.
- The promotion of unity and harmony among all sections of society in the villages;
- Such other matters as may be prescribed

7.13 SUMMARY

To increase peoples participation in development programmes, democratic decentralisation in the form of Panchayati Raj is adopted in India. It is a three-tier system consisting of Gram Panchayat, Panchayat Samiti and Zila Parishad. All the tires have well defined organisational structure as well as power and functions.

7.14 KEYWORDS

- **Democratic Decentralisation:** It means that the government which has derived its authority from the people redistributes it to some extent to the people for decision and action at the local level.
- **Gram Panchayat:** It is the lowest level tire of Panchayat. It is at

the village level.

- **Panchayat Samiti:** It is the middle-level tire of Panchayat. It is at the block level.
- **Zila Parishad:** It is the highest level tire of Panchayat. It is at the district level.

7.15 CHECK YOUR PROGRESS

1. What is Democratic Decentralisation?
2. Write the organizational structures of Gram Panchayat.
3. What is the organizational structure of Zila Parishad?
4. State 10 functions of Gram Panchayat.
5. State 10 functions of Panchayat Samiti.
6. State 10 functions of Zilla Parishad.
7. What is Gram Sabha ?

CHAPTER 8

Agricultural Development Programmes

8.0 OBJECTIVES

This chapter helps the students to understand different agricultural development programmes launched in India after independence. After completion of the unit, students will be able to:

1. Describe the Intensive Agricultural District Programme (IADP), its objectives and salient features.
2. State the High Yielding Varieties Programme (HYVP), its objectives and salient features.
3. Mention the Institute Village Linkage Programme (IVLP), its objectives and salient features.
4. Narrate the Watershed Development Programme, its objectives and salient features
5. Explain the National Agricultural Technology Programme (NATP), its objectives and salient features.
6. Describe the National Agricultural Innovation Project (NAIP), its objectives and salient features.
7. Explain the Agricultural Technology Information Center (ATIC), its objectives and salient features.
8. State the Agricultural Technology Management Agency (ATMA), its objectives and salient features.

8.1 INTRODUCTION

Agriculture is a vital part of the economy of any country, and its development is critical to the development of the country's economy as a whole. The Grow More Food Campaign (GMFC) was India's first organized effort to increase food production. It was launched in 1943. After independence, due attention has been given for the development of the public extension system in India. The GMFC was evaluated in 1952 by a government-appointed committee. One of the recommendations of the committee was that an extension agency should be set up for rural work which would reach every farmer and assist in the coordinated development of rural life. It was out of this background and experience that India's Community Development Programme (CDP) was initiated in 1952. Initially, the CDP was introduced in 55 project areas. But demand for expansion of CDP led to another scheme called National Extension Service which was launched in 1953. The large-scale food deficits of the late 1950s compelled the national Government to rethink its comprehensive rural development strategy and to concentrate solely on increasing food production. This was the beginning of the intensive approach through the Intensive Agricultural District Programme (IADP) in 1960. After that, some more programmes were launched for agricultural development. Some of the important programmes are discussed below.

8.2 INTENSIVE AGRICULTURAL DISTRICT PROGRAMME (IADP)

The Intensive Agricultural District Programme (IADP), was launched in the country from kharif, 1960. Initially, this was started with 7 districts (Thanjavur, West Godavari, Sahabad, Raipur, Aligarh, Ludhiana and Pali.). This programme was also popularly known as "package programme".

Objectives

1. The immediate goal was to achieve rapid increases in agricultural production through a concentration of financial, technical, extension and administrative resources.
2. Its aim, in the long run, is to achieve a self-generating 'breakthrough' in productivity and raise the production potential by stimulating the human and physical process of change.
3. The programme was also intended to provide lessons for extending such intense agricultural production programmes to other areas.

Salient Features

1. Provided factors of production simultaneously, timely and adequately to farmers
2. Essential inputs like fertilizer etc. were made available 100 per cent of the requirement
3. Credit was provided to any farmer who joined the programme and had the potential to get increased yield.
4. More agricultural and cooperatives staffs were posted.
5. Provisions were made for composite demonstration instead of single factor demonstration
6. The training was conducted periodically for staff.
7. Analysis and evolution were done regularly.

Achievement

1. Objectives were fulfilled for which it operated.
2. The basic concept of concentration had emerged as the foundation of India's present strategy of agricultural development.
3. Popularised High Yielding Variety programme
4. Greatly enhanced the use of technical inputs.

The spectacular results obtained in IADP resulted in the launching of the Intensive Agricultural Area Programme (IAAP) in March 1964. It covered large areas of the country at less cost and reduced staff strength.

8.3 HIGH YIELDING VARIETIES PROGRAMME (HYVP)

The Intensive Agricultural District Programme (IADP) and Intensive Agricultural Area Programme (IAAP) were concerned with the package approach, and intensive agriculture and these programmes increase the food production to some extent. But in the later period, when the yield was stabilized, it could not meet the demand for food production and this experience directed the need of High Yielding Varieties Programme (HYVP). The HYVP was launched in Kharif 1966-67.

Objective

The sole objective of HYVP was to increase the total food production by utilizing high yielding seeds of selected crops. The selected crops were paddy, wheat, bajra, jowar and maize.

Salient Features

1. Supply of inputs like seeds, fertilizers and plant protection chemicals,
2. Supply of credit,
3. Cooperative marketing,
4. National Demonstration and
5. Training.

Achievement

1. Helped in attaining self- sufficiency and stopped the import of food grains.
2. Achieved some significant results, particularly in the areas of increasing production and the awareness to the cultivators about available means of increasing production like high yielding seeds, fertilizers and plant protection chemicals.

8.4 INSTITUTE VILLAGE LINKAGE PROGRAMME (IVLP)

The field investigations conducted in the last decade world over, clearly suggest that many modern technologies are simply inappropriate for the specific conditions of small-farm production systems which are highly diverse in nature and are largely influenced both by socio-economic as well as biophysical factors. Social and biological scientists are now becoming aware of the existing complex farming systems and understand the reasons for non-adoption of technologies by resource-poor farmers. They have, therefore, emphasized the need for participation of farmers in technology selection management process for the generation of appropriate technologies.

A more holistic approach in terms of diagnosis of problems, identification of technological interventions based on farmers knowledge and technology identification for various production systems is called for to generate appropriate technologies. It is in this concept a programme captioned Technology Assessment and Refinement through Institute Village Linkage Programme (TAR-IVLP) was evolved to address the above elements to arrive at appropriate technologies. The programme was initiated on a pilot basis in 1995. It was implemented in 42 centres of selected ICAR institutes and SAUs The programme got its fillip and momentum since 1999 when it was brought under the fold of NATP as a part.

Objectives of IVLP

1. To introduce technological interventions with an emphasis on stability and sustainability along with productivity and profitability taking into account environmental issues in well endowed and small production systems.
2. To introduce and integrate appropriate technologies to increase productivity with a marketed surplus in commercial and off-farm production systems.
3. To monitor the socio-economic impact of technological interventions for different production systems.
4. To identify extrapolation domain for new technology/ technology modules based on environmental characterization as at meso and mega levels.

Salient Feature

1. **Paradigm:** Two important paradigms considered in the pilot project were:
   a) First, technology has to be assessed and refined before they are transferred, and second, a programme approach involving various technological components relevant to the farmers under varying agro-ecological conditions.
2. **Selection of operational area**: A village is the unit of operation of TAR-IVLP. Selection of suitable village or a cluster of villages covering about 1000 farm families and having a representation of various production systems is of paramount importance.
3. **Constitution of a multidisciplinary team of scientists:** The project is implemented by Central Agricultural Research Institutes/State Agricultural Universities through a

multidisciplinary core team of scientists numbering 4-5 from the implementing institution led by a Team Leader. (Principal Investigator). The TAR-IVLP also envisages an optional team of scientists drawn from other institutes to look into specific issues.

4. **Agro-ecosystem analysis (AESA):** The AESA of the village using PRA techniques was the first step towards launching the programme. It provided information on resource availability, production practices, interaction within and amongst various resources and enterprises on a spatial and temporal basis.
5. **Problem diagnosis and technology intervention:** Based on the information elicited from AESA and the legitimization through focused group discussion, problems of various enterprises in terms of biophysical and socio-economic causes were identified. The identified problems were prioritized, and possible technological interventions were assessed in a focused group discussion with farmers and scientists.
6. **Action Plan for technology assessment and refinement:** The technological interventions contemplated were categorized down into specific action plans in terms of On-Farm Trials/ demonstration, treatments, local checks, number of trials, plot size, critical inputs etc. Action plans were prepared, keeping in view the AESA and in consultation with farmers. The technologies were evaluated not solely in terms of their technical/economic performance, but also in terms of their conformity to socio-economic and cultural circumstances, goals and needs with the active participation of farmers.
7. **Site committee meetings:** Action plans were also discussed in the site committee meetings to improve the nature of interventions. Site committee was constituted for proper implementation, including site selection and project submission considering the guidelines of ICAR. Site committee meetings were held to advise the TAR-IVLP core team on the selection, modifications and approval of techno-interventions and action plan in the adopted villages and overall review of the project.
8. **Monitoring and Evaluation:** The goals of this component are to measure the scale of success. The review team was

constituted comprising of subject experts for this purpose. The peer review team visited the TAR-IVLP villages to monitor the progress of the project and made specific recommendations. The progress of TAR-IVLP was also monitored through organizing workshops and Agro-Ecosystem Director visits.

Achievements

Though detailed systematic study to evaluate the performance of IVLP is not done, but few studies reported that:

1. There is an increase in yield level in the IVLP site in respect to paddy, wheat, gram in some areas.
2. Supply of quality seeds assured good yield in some project site in case of a gram, barley, wheat etc.
3. Reaching of new technologies to farmer's level through demonstrations conducted under IVLP.
4. Assessments of existing technologies are also successfully done in some IVLP site and made refinement based on farmer's experiences.

8.5 WATERSHED DEVELOPMENT PROGRAMME

The Department of Land Resources in the Ministry of Rural Development is administering three area-based watershed programmes for development of wastelands/degraded lands, namely, Drought Prone Areas Programmes (DPAP), Desert Development Programme (DDP) and Integrated Wastelands Development Programme (IWDP) to check the diminishing productivity of wasteland and loss of natural resources.

The DPAP was launched in 1973-74 to tackle the special problems faced by those areas that are constantly afflicted by drought conditions. DDP was launched in 1977-78 to mitigate the adverse effects of desertification. DDP and DPAP were brought into a watershed mode in 1987. IWDP has been under implementation since 1989. The projects under the IWDP are generally sanctioned in areas that are not covered under DDP or DPAP. All these programmes were brought under the Guidelines for Watershed Development with effect from 1st April.1995. From 1st April 2003, IWDP, DDP and DPAP are implemented under Harywali programmes. However, the projects which were sanctioned before the date are implemented as per Guidelines for Watershed Development Projects.

Objectives

1. Developing wastelands/degraded lands, drought-prone and desert areas on a watershed basis, keeping in view the land capability, site-conditions and local needs.
2. Promoting the overall economic development and improving the socio-economic condition of the resource-poor and disadvantaged sections inhabiting the programme areas.
3. Mitigating the adverse effects of extreme climatic conditions such as drought and desertification on crops, human and livestock population for their improvement.
4. Restoring ecological balance by harnessing, conserving and developing natural resources, i.e. land, water and vegetative cover.

Salient Feature

1. Each watershed areas cover 500 ha.
2. In case a watershed falls under two villages, it is divided into two sub-watershed areas confined to the designated villages.
3. Watersheds having a large population of SC/ST dependents on it are selected first.
4. Self- help group, user group etc. are formed from the direct and indirect beneficiaries.
5. Sought people's participation in the programmes in case of cash, raw material, labour etc.
6. At villages level, gram panchayat is fully involved in implementing the programmes.
7. Population below the poverty line, particularly the marginalised groups like marginal farmers, landless labourers, especially women, are the target beneficiaries.
8. DRDA implemented the programme through Project Implementing Agencies.

Achievements

1. Improvement in groundwater level, cultivated area and productivity of Land
2. The decrease in soil erosion, runoff loss and silting of ponds, tanks and dams
3. Increase in availability of fodder, milk production, fuel and employment
4. Improvement in the overall socio-economic status of rural people living in/around watershed areas
5. Watershed Villages" were seen to have developed sufficient drought sustenance capacity.

National Watershed Development Project for Rainfed Areas (NWDRPA)

The National Watershed Development Project for Rainfed Areas (NWDRPA) is a centrally sponsored mandated scheme, and has the following broad criteria:

1. <30% area is irrigated,
2. <750 mm average rainfall (30-years),
3. No other schemes have been implemented.
4. Size of a watershed for this scheme is »10000 ha (100 km^2), and may not correspond to the physical geographer's concept of a natural watershed.

Government of India sponsored the NWDPRA in the country for scientific land use through the development of the integrated farming system on the principles of watershed management where the arable area under assured means of irrigation is less than 30%.

Objectives

This project aims at:

1. Conservation, development, sustainable management of natural resources, including their use.
2. Enhancement of Agricultural Productivity and Production in a sustainable manner.

3. Restoration of Ecological balance in the degraded and fragile rainfed Eco-system by greening these areas through an appropriate mix of trees, shrubs and grasses.
4. Reduction in a regional disparity between irrigated and rainfed areas.
5. Creation of sustained employment opportunities for the rural community, including the landless.

Hariyali Programme

To involve village communities in the implementation of watershed projects under all the area development programmes namely, Integrated Wastelands Development Programme (IWDP), Drought Prone Areas Programme (DPAP) and Desert Development Programme (DDP), the Guidelines for Watershed Development were adopted w.e.f. 1st April 1995, and subsequently revised in August 2001. To further simplify procedures and involve the Panchayat Raj Institutions (PRIs) more meaningfully in planning, implementation and management of economic development activities in rural areas, these new Guidelines called 'Guidelines for Hariyali' are being issued.

Applicability

New projects under the area development programmes shall be implemented in accordance with the Guidelines for Hariyali with effect from 1.4.2003. Projects under DPAP and DDP will be taken up in the blocks identified under the respective programme and projects under IWDP shall generally be taken up in the remaining blocks. Projects sanctioned prior to this date shall continue to be implemented as per the Guidelines of 2001.

Objectives

The objectives of projects under HARIYALI will be:

1. Harvesting every drop of rainwater for purposes of irrigation, plantations including horticulture and floriculture, pasture development, fisheries etc. to create sustainable sources of income for the village community as well as for drinking water supplies.

2. Ensuring overall development of rural areas through the Gram Panchayats and creating regular sources of income for the Panchayats from rainwater harvesting and management.
3. Employment generation, poverty alleviation, community empowerment and development of human and other economic resources of the rural areas.
4. Mitigating the adverse effects of extreme climatic conditions such as drought and desertification on crops, human and livestock population for the overall improvement of rural areas.
5. Restoring ecological balance by harnessing, conserving and developing natural resources, i.e. land, water, vegetative cover especially plantations.
6. Encouraging village community towards sustained community action for the operation and maintenance of assets created and further development of the potential of the natural resources in the watershed.
7. Promoting the use of simple, easy and affordable technological solutions and institutional arrangements that make use of, and build upon, local technical knowledge and available materials.

8.6 NATIONAL AGRICULTURAL TECHNOLOGY PROGRAMME (NATP)

After the WTO, there is a rapid global change in agricultural trade. There is also an emerging need to radically reform the extension system to meet the above challenges. Therefore, National Agricultural Technology Programme was conceived as a pilot project. It was launched in November 1998. It was an initiative of the Government of India with World Bank assistance.

Objective

The overall objective of NATP was to revitalize the agricultural technology generation, assessment, refinement and dissemination systems. More specifically, objectives were:

1. Increase the quality and type of technologies disseminated through
   a) location specific technology development
   b) diversification and intensification of farming systems

2. use of sustainability enhancing technologies
   a) Enable research and extension system to become demand driven and responsible for solving problems of farmers.
   b) Strengthening research -extension-farmers (R-E-F) linkages
   c) Increase the financial sustainability of the system
   d) Shared ownership of Agricultural technology system (ATS) by key stakeholders

Salient Features

1. It had three components. These were as follows:
   a) ICAR organization and management reforms
   b) expansion of location-specific research on a production system
   c) testing of innovations in technology dissemination
2. The Innovation in Technology Dissemination (ITD) component of the project aimed at addressing key constraints in technology generation, validation and dissemination by introducing new institutional models and operational reform process in selected states.
3. Seven states were selected for this pilot project. These were Bihar, Andhra Pradesh, Himachal Pradesh, Jharkhand, Maharastra, Orissa and Punjab. The project was pilot tested in four districts each of the above-mentioned states.
4. Under NATP, some institutional innovations were made under ITD in each project district. These were as follows:
   a) Establishment of decentralized district level autonomous institutions named ATMA (Agricultural Technology Management Agency)
   b) Establishing FIAC (Farm Information and Advisory Centre) at the block level.
   c) Establishment of state-level agricultural extension management training institutions named SAMETI (State Agricultural Extension Management and Training Institutes).
   d) Evolution of state-level coordination and policy-making body named IDWG (Inter-Departmental Working Group).

5. With an objective to address the expanding role of extension, certain operational reforms processes were initiated in the project districts like strategic planning, bottom-up planning, promotion of farmer interest group and farmers organization, farming system approach, decentralized decision making, farmer participation research, market-led production, sequential extension interventions, cost and resource sharing, IT and communication support, public-private partnership, techno-managerial focus, team approach and farmers focused and farmer accountable extension.

Achievement

1. Introduction of the ATMA model by the entire country as an extension reform process.
2. Establishment of SAMETI by various states
3. Empowerment of the farming community
4. Formation of Farmers Interest Groups and Farmers Organisations at different states.
5. Introduction of Public-Private Partnership in the extension system.
6. Introducing the group approach of extension
7. Introduction of bottom-up planning.
8. Under NATP extension system was found to be cost-effective and sustainable.
9. Introduced Strategic Research and Extension Plan (SREP) at district levels.

8.7 NATIONAL AGRICULTURAL INNOVATION PROJECT (NAIP)

NAIP has been envisaged for facilitating the accelerated and sustainable transformation of agriculture in support of poverty alleviation and income generation through technological innovations by the public research organizations in partnership with farmer's group, the private sector, the civil society organizations and other stakeholders. The total budget is allocated under this project is approximately Rs.1150 crores (US$250 million) out of which the World Bank would fund Rs. 920 crores (US$200 million) as credit and the government of India would fund Rs.230 crores (US$50 million). The project is for 6 years (July 2006 to June 2012).

Objectives

1. To give agricultural research and technology development system, an explicit development and business perspective through innovative models. In other words, the agricultural research system should be able to support agriculture as a business venture and also as a means of security for the livelihood of the rural Indian while maintaining excellence in science.
2. To make the national agricultural research system, a pluralistic system where every stakeholder has a role to play.
3. Create a well-defined partnership grouped with clear common goals and understanding of sharing responsibilities and benefits.
4. Develop well-tested models for application of agricultural research and technology for the profitability of farming, income generation and poverty alleviation.

Salient Feature

NAIP is to function through the following four components

1. ICAR as the catalyzing agent for the management of change in the Indian National Agricultural Research System and would involve:
   a) information, communication and dissemination systems which support interactions and dialogue among the stakeholders
   b) capacity building
   c) business planning and development for agricultural technologies and knowledge
   d) policy analysis including that for gender concerns, visioning and market intelligence analysis for supporting the policymakers on the one hand and the farmer on the other hand.
2. Research on production to consumption system (PCS) and

would involve:

a) the PCS is a system which involves the entire set of agencies, materials, activities, technologies and services and instructions involved from the stage of inputs to harvesting of a particular commodity and transforming it into a usable product and storing/marketing the final product. This entails a field to plate system.

b) rural income augmentation and employment generation through post-harvest processing and value addition, the building of rural agro-industries, export promotion and import substitution will receive thrust.

c) research for technology development and adoption needed for each link within a PCS will be addressed by each selected consortium.

3. **Research on sustainable rural livelihood security (SRLS):** In this area emphasis to be given are- on-farm research, for improving and developing to most suitable farming system and allied off-farm activities, in the less favorable environments, regions and groups so that the livelihood of rural poor improves through food, nutrition employment and income.

4. **Basic and strategic research in the frontier areas of agricultural sciences (BSR):** Area of activities would be

   a) genetic enhancement of plants
   b) genetic enhancement of animals
   c) natural resources management and IPM
   d) novel value addition, processing and storage methods for agricultural products and byproducts
   e) development of state of the art animal disease surveillance and control system

5. One hundred fifty disadvantaged districts have been identified by the Planning Commission covering 27 States and 13 agro-climatic zones under NAIP.

6. Formation of consortia to carry out the identified task.

8.8 AGRICULTURAL TECHNOLOGY INFORMATION CENTER (ATIC)

The primary goal of agricultural extension is to assist farming families in adapting their production and marketing strategies to rapidly changing social, political and economic conditions so that they can, in their long term, shape their lives according to their personal preferences and those of the community. The task of extension is to improve interactions with the Agriculture Knowledge System (AKS) so that farmers have optimum access to any information that could help them enhance their economic and social situation. To attain these objectives, the Indian Council of Agricultural Research initiated Transfer of Technology (TOT) projects through various means like Krishi Vigyan Kendras, and Institute-Village Linkage Programme Centres. Though the aforesaid TOT projects and their vast mechanisms are made to help and serve the farming community, some of the important needs of the farmers are not yet met:

The five important needs of the farmers are:

1. Awareness of and motivation to use improved technologies / management practices.
2. Advice on appropriate farm planning and resource management.
3. Practical farming skills relevant to new technologies / management practices.
4. Production inputs and credits and
5. Postharvest and marketing services to farmers to get a good price in competitive global agriculture.

Interestingly these needs of the farmers irrespective of their locations and farming practices are not realized by the existing transfer of technology projects. Hence a new and innovative transfer of technology mechanism named, Agricultural Technology Information Centre (ATIC) has been conceived and put into practice since 1998-99 under National Agricultural Technology Project (NATP) sponsored by World Bank and implemented through 40 ICAR Institutes and State Agricultural Universities (SAUs) located in various parts of the country.

Objectives

1. To provide a single window delivery system for the products

and species available from an institution to the farmers and other interested groups as a process of innovativeness in technology dissemination at the institute level;

2. To facilitate direct access to the farmers to the institutional resources available in terms of technology, advice, products, etc., for reducing dissemination losses; and to provide a mechanism for feedback from the users to the institute.

The salient feature of ATIC

1. ATIC is intended to provide all basic needs of the farmers through a single window service. This unique system not only serves the farmers but also other stakeholders of the farming practices to provide a solution to their location-specific problems and make available all the required technical information together with technology inputs and products for testing and use by them.
2. The rationale behind the establishment of ATIC has been:
    a) Providing diagnostic services for soil testing, plant and livestock health;
    b) Supplying research products such as seeds and other planting material, poultry strains, livestock breeds, fish seed, processed products, etc., emerging from the institution for testing and adaptation by various clientele;
    c) Disseminating information through published literature and communication materials as well as audio-visual aids; and
    d) Providing an opportunity to the institutes / SAUs to have resource generation through the sale of their technologies.
3. The inbuilt mechanism of ATIC ensures:
    a) Availability and accessibility of new technologies
    b) The relevance of new technologies
    c) Responsiveness of new technologies to the needs of different categories of farmers
    d) Varied requirements for different categories of farmers and
    e) Sustainability of such unit within overall institutional framework.

Achievement of ATIC

No details study is made to evaluate the achievements of ATIC. But some tangible achievements are observed in case of ATIC. These are

1. All recent technologies are now available to farmers through single window system at ATICs
2. Provides services to various categories of farmers through the single window system.
3. Supply of quality inputs to farmers.
4. Provides solution based on diagnosis to farmers' problems etc.

8.9 AGRICULTURAL TECHNOLOGY MANAGEMENT AGENCY (ATMA)

The institutional mechanism in the form of Agricultural Technology Management Agency (ATMA) at district level was pilot tested under Innovations in Technology Dissemination (ITD) component of National Agricultural Technology Project (NATP) in seven states and 28 districts from 1998 to 2004. Extension Reforms were introduced during 2005-06 by the Department of Agriculture and Cooperation (DAC), Ministry of Agriculture, Government of India as a major intervention in addressing the constraints as observed in T and V and post T and V system by making the extension system farmer driven and farmer accountable through process and institutional reforms mechanism. ATMA is a component of this extension reforms and all state establish ATMA at the district level.

ATMA can receive funds directly (Government of India/States, Membership fees, beneficiaries' contribution, etc.). Local research and extension priorities are set through Strategic Research and Extension Plans (SREPs), which are developed by using participatory methodologies such as Participatory Rural Appraisal (PRA). ATMA is being supported by a Governing Board (GB) and a Management Committee (MC). Under each ATMA, Farm Information and Advisory Center (FIACs) are created at the block level. It consists of two bodies, namely Farmer Advisory Committee (FAC) and Block Technology Team (BTT). The FAC is a body of farmer representatives (11-15 members representing various enterprises and socioeconomic strata). Key functions of FACs are to act as an agency for providing farmer feedback mechanism, help set block extension priorities and recommend resource allocation across programme areas, recommend Block Action Plan for approval of ATMA Governing Body, review and provide advise to each implementation unit at block level and help in formation of Farmer Interest Groups at block level and below. The BTT, on the other hand, is a group of technical advisors operating at block level representing agriculture and allied sectors. It is an Inter-Departmental Team of Agriculture and Line Departments operating at the block level. The key functions of Block Technology Team are to facilitate formation of Farmers Interest Group (FIGs)/Farmers Organisation (FOs) at the block level and below, operationalize the SREP in each block and move towards single window extension system, help district core team in up gradation of SREP, prepare Block Action Plan detailing extension activities to be undertaken, and coordinate the implementation of extension programmes detailed in the Block Action Plan. FAC and BTT act as a planning and operational arm of ATMA. Commodity-oriented Farmer Interest Groups (FIGs) and SHGs are promoted at block/village level to make the technology generation/dissemination farmer driven and farmer accountable. In order to address the extension needs of these groups, ATMA has established close linkages with various players operating at cutting edge level viz. public, private, NGOs, Para extension workers, input dealers, etc. In order to provide needed HRD support in innovative areas of extension delivery, a State Agricultural Management and Extension Training Institute (SAMETI) has been established.

Objectives

1. To identify location specific needs of the farming community for a farming system based agricultural development
2. To set up priorities for sustainable agricultural development with a farming system approach
3. To draw plans for production based system activities to be undertaken by farmers /ultimate users
4. To execute plans through line departments, training institutions, NGOs, farmers organization and allied institutions

5. To coordinate efforts being made by various line departments, NGOs, organizations of the farmers and allied institutions.
6. To strengthen research- extension-farmers linkages in the district and to promote collaboration and coordination between various state-funded technical departments.
7. To facilitate the empowerment of farmers/producers through assistance for their increased participation in planning, marketing, technology dissemination and agro-processing etc.
8. To facilitate market interventions for value addition to farm produce.

Salient Features

1. ATMA is established at the district level as an autonomous institution providing flexible working environment involving all the stakeholders in planning and implementation of extension activities.
2. ATMA is a unique district level institution, which caters to activities in agriculture and allied sectors adopting a farming systems approach and convergence of programmes of related departments.
3. Local research and extension priorities are set through Strategic Research and Extension Plans (SREPs), which are developed using participatory methodologies.
4. ATMA is registered under the "Societies Registration Act of 1860" that has considerable operational flexibility.
5. It operates under the guidance of a Governing Board (GB) that determines programme priorities and assesses programme impact.
6. The executive head of ATMA is known as the Project Director (PD) and reports directly to the ATMA Governing Board.
7. One of the most important activities undertaken by ATMA is to prepare Strategic Research and Extension Plan (SREP), which consist of detailed information about agriculture and allied sectors in the district.
8. The purpose of preparation of SREP is to identify research and extension needs of the district. This helps in undertaking only those extension activities which are needed by farmers in the

district.

9. SREP is prepared with the full participation of farmers and their representatives at a different level. Technical officers of agriculture and allied departments as well as from KVKs and other research institutions fully participate in the preparation of SREPs.
10. Based on the research-extension strategies given in the SREPs, block/ district level plans are developed by ATMA institutions.
11. The concept of ATMA envisages a paradigm shift from 'top-down' to 'bottom up' in the planning and implementation of agricultural development programmes.

Achievements

1. It is proved as a cost-effective extension system
2. Peoples' participation is more in this approach
3. Introduction of NGO in extension system particularly in case of farmer's mobilization
4. Involvement of women in agricultural development is increased
5. Bottom-up planning for agricultural development ensured a quick solution for many farmers' problem
6. Farmers' organisations are formed which empower the farmers.

8.10 SOME OTHER IMPORTANT PROGRAMMES

Besides these above-mentioned programmes, some other important programmes related to agricultural development are also implemented in India. Though these are not part of the syllabus for the interest of the students, some selected programmes are mentioned below.

A. Small Farmer's Development Agency (SFDA)

During the green revolution, all the small farmers were not benefited from the Green Revolution. Accordingly, the fourth Five-year plan laid special emphasis on enabling the small farmers to participate in the process of development and share the benefits.

To achieve the objective, the plan provided for the initiation of a project, namely Small Farmer's Development Agency (SFDA) scheme, which was sanctioned during 1970-71. But the actual implementation started only during 1971-72. It is an autonomous agency registered under the Societies Registration Act 1860. It is established at the district level. Initially, it was a central level scheme until 1978-79, later it becomes a joint venture of central and state government.

The aims of the SFDA are to identify the problems of the small farmers, to prepare appropriate programmes to overcome them and ensure the availability of inputs and credit. In all, about 50 SFDA projects have been established throughout the country under the Fourth Five-Year Plan, and Rs.68 crores were allotted for these projects during the Fourth Plan.

B. Marginal Farmers and Agricultural Labourers Projects (MFAL)

This scheme was also launched in 1970-71. Its objective is to assist the marginal cultivators in making the maximum productive use of their small holdings by undertaking horticulture, animal husbandry and dairying. Efforts are also to be directed towards bringing in larger incomes by channelling credits, improved inputs and improved practices. Under this scheme, 41 projects were scheduled to be established throughout the country in the Fourth Five-Year Plan to cover farmers having holdings of not more than one hectare and agricultural labourers having a homestead and earning half or more of their income from agricultural wages. Each Project aimed at covering about 20,000 households during the Fourth Five-Year Plan, of which about two-thirds would be from the marginal farmers and the rest from agricultural labourers. On the recommendation of the National Commission on Agriculture (1976), MFAL was merged with SFDA

C. Rashtriya Krishi Vikas Yojana (RKVY)

Economic reforms initiated since 1991 have put the Indian economy on a higher growth trajectory. The annual growth rate in the total Gross Domestic Product (GDP) has accelerated from below 6 per cent during the initial years of reforms to more than 8 per cent in recent years. The Planning Commission, in its approach paper to the Eleventh Five-Year-plan, has stated that a 9 per cent growth rate in GDP would be feasible during the Eleventh Plan period. However, Agriculture that accounted for more than 30 per cent of total GDP at the beginning of reforms failed to maintain its pre-reform growth. On the contrary, it witnessed a sharp deceleration in growth after the mid-1990s. This happened despite the fact that agricultural productivity in most of the states was quite low as it were, and the potential for the growth of agriculture was high.

The GDP of agriculture increased annually at more than 3 per cent during the 1980s. Since the Ninth Five-Year Plan (1996 to 2001-02), India has been targeting a growth rate of more than 4 per cent in agriculture, but the actual achievement has been much below the target. More than 50 per cent of the workforce of the country still depends upon agriculture for its livelihood. Slow growth in Agriculture and allied sectors can lead to acute stress in the economy because the population dependent upon this sector is still very large. A major cause behind the slow growth in agriculture is the consistent decrease in investments in the sector by the state governments. While public and private investments are increasing manifold in sectors such as infrastructure, similar investments are not forthcoming in Agriculture and allied sectors, leading to distress in the community of farmers, especially that of the small and marginal segment. Hence the need for incentivising states that increase their investments in the Agriculture and allied sectors has been felt.

Concerned by the slow growth in the Agriculture and allied sectors, the National Development Council (NDC), in its meeting held on 29th May 2007 resolved that a special Additional Central Assistance Scheme (RKVY) be launched. The NDC resolved that agricultural development strategies must be reoriented to meet the needs of farmers and called upon the Central and State governments to evolve a strategy to rejuvenate agriculture. The NDC reaffirmed its commitment to achieving 4 per cent annual growth in the agricultural sector during the 11th plan.

Basic Features of RKVY

The RKVY aims at achieving 4% annual growth in the agriculture sector during the XI Plan period, by ensuring holistic development of Agriculture and allied sectors. The main objectives of the scheme are:

1. To incentivise the states so as to increase public investment in Agriculture and allied sectors.
2. To provide flexibility and autonomy to states in the process of planning and executing Agriculture and allied sector schemes.
3. To ensure the preparation of agriculture plans for the districts and the states based on agro-climatic conditions, availability of technology and natural resources.
4. To ensure that the local needs/crops/priorities are better reflected in the agricultural plans of the states.
5. To achieve the goal of reducing the yield gaps in important crops, through focused interventions.
6. To maximize returns to the farmers in Agriculture and allied sectors.
7. To bring about quantifiable changes in the production and productivity of various components of Agriculture and allied sectors by addressing them in a holistic manner.

These guidelines are applicable to all the States and Union Territories that fulfil the eligibility conditions.

The RKVY is a State Plan Scheme

1. Since the RKVY is applicable to the entire State Plan for Agriculture and allied sectors, and seeks to encourage convergence with schemes like NREGS, SGSY and BRGF, the Planning Commission and the Ministry of Agriculture will together examine the States ' overall Plan proposals for Agriculture and allied sectors as part of the Annual Plan approval exercise.
2. Once a state becomes eligible for the RKVY, the quantum of assistance and the process of subsequent allocation to the state will be in accordance with the parameters and the respective weights
3. It will be permissible for the states to initiate specific projects with definite timelines, and clear objectives for Agriculture and

allied sectors excluding forestry and wildlife, and plantations (i.e., Coffee, Tea and Rubber). For this purpose, the RKVY would be available to the states in two distinct streams. At least 75% of the allocated amount shall be proposed under Stream-I for specific projects. The amount under Stream- II, will be available for strengthening the existing state sector schemes and filling the resource gaps.

4. A State Level Sanctioning Committee (SLSC) headed by the Chief Secretary of the state will have the authority to sanction specific projects under the Stream-I. The Government of India's representative shall participate in the SLSC meetings, and the quorum shall not be complete without the presence of at least one official from the Government of India.
5. There may arise a situation when a particular state becomes ineligible to avail of the funds under the RKVY in a subsequent year due to its lowered expenditure on Agriculture and allied sectors. If this were to happen, the states should be required to commit their own resources for completing the sanctioned projects/schemes under the RKVY.
6. The pattern of funding is 100% Central grant, and the eventual goal is that the additional investments made through the RKVY scheme will lead to at least 4% growth in agriculture.

Areas of focus under RKVY

The components / activities which would be eligible for project-based assistance under the Stream-I of the RKVY are elaborated below. This is an indicative list; the states may choose other components/activities. The components for the RKVY could cover the following:

1. ***Integrated development of major food crops such as wheat, paddy, coarse cereals, minor millets, pulses, oilseeds*:** Assistance can be provided for making available certified/ HYV seeds to farmers; production of breeder seed; purchase of breeder seed from institutions such as ICAR, public sector seed corporations, production of foundation seed; production of certified seed; seed treatment; Farmers Field Schools at demonstration sites; training of farmers etc. Similar support

would be provided for development of other crops such as sugarcane, cotton or any other crop/variety that may be of importance to the state.

2. ***Agriculture mechanization*:** Assistance would be provided for farm mechanization efforts, especially for improved and gender friendly tools, implements and machinery. Specific agricultural mechanization projects oriented toward enhancing farm productivity can be considered under this scheme. However, tractors are not covered under the scheme.
3. ***Activities related to the enhancement of soil health*:** This would include efficient quality control of inputs, including strengthening of laboratories and enhancing soil health. Assistance can be provided to the farmers for distributing soil health cards; micronutrient demonstration; training of farmers for promotion of organic farming including printing of publicity/utility literature; assistance to the state government to strengthen existing soil testing and fertilizer testing laboratories and setting up new ones; amelioration of soils affected with conditions such as alkalinity and acidity.
4. ***Development of rainfed farming systems in and outside watershed areas, as also Integrated development of watershed areas, wastelands, river valleys:*** Assistance for development of land as also assistance for horticulture, generating livelihoods for farmers Below the Poverty Line (BPL).
5. ***Support to State seed farms*:** State farms that are used for both research and seed production purposes may be provided funds in a project mode covering aspects such as land development, creation of irrigation facilities, upgrading technology, etc. However, new land acquisition is not permitted.
6. ***Integrated Pest Management schemes*:** This would include training of farmers through Farm Field Schools etc. on pest management practices; printing of literature/ other awareness programmes.
7. ***Encouraging non-farm activities*:** Assistance to agri-entreprenuers / agri-graduates to set up agri-clinics / agri-business centres.

8. ***Strengthening of Market Infrastructure and marketing development:*** Assistance for setting up of cold storages, cold chains, godowns, the formation of farmer's SHGs, setting up collection centre etc. Assistance to PRIs/SHGs in promoting collection and sale to mandis/government agencies.
9. ***Strengthening of Infrastructure to promote Extension Services:*** This would include new initiatives for skill development and training in the farming community and to revamp the existing State agricultural extension systems.
10. ***Activities relating to enhancement of horticultural production and popularization of micro irrigation systems*****:** Assistance will be available for nursery development, horticulture activities including marketing and drip/sprinkler irrigation.
11. ***Animal husbandry and fisheries development activities*****:** Assistance will be available for improvement in fodder production, genetic upgradation of cattle and buffaloes, enhancement of milk production, enlarging raw material base for leather industry, improvement in livestock health, poultry development, development of small ruminants and enhanced fish production.
12. ***Special schemes for beneficiaries of land reforms*****:** Assistance will be available for improving the net minimum income of this category of beneficiaries. Beneficiaries of land reforms are usually small and marginal farmers. Making their agriculture viable will be possible only when capital investments on land development, irrigation, high-technology infrastructure in emerging areas such as floriculture, horticulture, seed production, etc. are made. Specific projects for groups of such beneficiaries can be taken up with provision for common infrastructure.
13. ***Undertaking concept to completion projects:*** Undertaking specific projects under agriculture/horticulture/ allied sectors in a concept to completion mode with attention given to all the components such as crop production, technology induction, farmer training, forward and backward linkages, either entirely in the state sector or in partnership with the private sector, where necessary and possible, is permitted

under the scheme. Beneficiaries under such projects should, however, predominately be BPL farmers. Projects in risk-prone, underdeveloped, agriculturally distressed, remote, hilly and tribal areas are especially encouraged.

14. ***Grant support to the State Government institutions that promote agriculture/horticulture:*** Wherever state-level institutions that work for promoting agriculture/horticulture/allied sectors require one-time grant support for their functioning/strengthening, such support can be provided.
15. ***Study tours of farmers:*** Study tours of farmers to places of interest to them, especially to research institutions etc.
16. ***Organic and bio-fertilizers:*** Support for decentralized production at the village level and their marketing, etc. This will include vermicomposting and introduction of superior technologies for better production.
17. ***Innovative schemes:*** The above list is not exhaustive. Therefore, schemes that are important for agriculture, horticulture and allied sector development, but cannot be categorized under (a) to (p) can also be proposed, as innovative schemes.

Operationalisation of RKVY

The State Agriculture Department shall be the nodal department for the implementation of the scheme. For administrative convenience and ease of implementation, the state governments may identify, or create an exclusive agency for implementing the scheme on the fast-track. Even where such an Agency is created/designated, the entire responsibility of ensuring that the RKVY is properly implemented will be that of the Agriculture Department only. In a situation where the states notify a Nodal agency, the release of funds may be done by the Centre directly to the Agency.

(Source: http://agri.gujarat.gov.in/download/rkvy.pdf)

D. National Horticulture Mission

National Horticulture Mission (NHM) is implemented in all the States and Union Territories of India except the North Eastern States, Himachal Pradesh, Jammu & Kashmir and Uttaranchal (for which a separate Technology Mission for integrated development of horticulture exists) to promote holistic growth of the horticulture sector covering fruits, vegetables, root & tuber crops, mushroom, spices, flowers, aromatic plants, cashew and cocoa. This is a Centrally sponsored scheme in which the Government of India shall provide 100% assistance to the State Missions during the Tenth Plan. During the XI Plan, the Government of India assistance will be 85% with 15% contribution by the State Governments.

Objectives

The main objectives of the Mission are:

1. To provide holistic growth of the horticulture sector through an area based regionally differentiated strategies which include research, technology promotion, extension, post-harvest management, processing and marketing, in consonance with comparative advantage of each State/region and its diverse agro-climatic feature;
2. To enhance horticulture production, improve nutritional security and income support to farm households;
3. To establish convergence and synergy among multiple on-going and planned programmes for horticulture development;
4. To promote, develop and disseminate technologies, through a seamless blend of traditional wisdom and modern scientific knowledge;
5. To create opportunities for employment generation for skilled and unskilled persons, especially unemployed youth.

Strategy

To achieve the above objectives, the mission would adopt the following strategies:

1. Ensure an end-to-end holistic approach covering production, post-harvest management, processing and marketing to assure appropriate returns to growers/producers;
2. Promote R&D technologies for production, post-harvest management and processing;
3. Enhance acreage, coverage, and productivity through:
   a) Diversification, from traditional crops to plantations, orchards, vineyards, flower and vegetable gardens;

   b) Extension of appropriate technology to the farmers for high-tech horticulture cultivation and precision farming.
4. Assist setting up post-harvest facilities such as pack house, ripening chamber, cold storages, Controlled Atmosphere (CA) storages etc., processing units for value addition and marketing infrastructure;
5. Adopt a coordinated approach and promotion of partnership, convergence and synergy among R&D, processing and marketing agencies in public as well as private sectors, at the National, Regional, State and sub-State levels;
6. Where appropriate and feasible, promote the National Dairy Development Board (NDDB) model of cooperatives to ensure support and adequate returns to farmers;
7. Promote capacity-building and Human Resource Development at all levels.

(Source: http://www.indg.in/agriculture/rural-employment-schemes/national-horticulture-mission/nhm-guidelines-english.pdf)

E. National Food Security Mission (NFSM)

The growth in food grain production has stagnated during the recent past, while the consumption need of the growing population is increasing. To meet the growing food grain demand, the National Development Council (NDC) in its 53rd meeting held on 29th May, 2007 adopted a resolution to launch a Food Security Mission comprising rice, wheat and pulses to increase the production of rice by 10 million tons, wheat by 8 million tons and pulses by 2 million tons by the end of the Eleventh Plan (2011-12). Accordingly, A Centrally Sponsored Scheme, 'National Food Security Mission', has been launched from August 2007 to operationalize the above-mentioned resolution.

Objective

The major objective of this scheme is to increase the production and productivity of wheat, rice and pulses on a sustainable basis so as to ensure food security of the country. The approach is to bridge the yield gap in respect of these crops through the dissemination of improved technologies and farm management practices. More specifically, the objectives are:

1. Increasing production of rice, wheat and pulses through area expansion and productivity enhancement in a sustainable manner in the identified districts of the country;
2. Restoring soil fertility and productivity at the individual farm level;
3. Creation of employment opportunities; and
4. Enhancing farm level economy (i.e. farm profits) to restore confidence amongst the farmers.

Strategy

To achieve the above objectives, the Mission would adopt the following strategies:

1. Implementation in a mission mode through active engagement of all the stakeholders at various levels.
2. Management including micronutrients, soil amendments, IPM and resource conservation technologies along with the capacity building of farmers.
3. The flow of fund would be closely monitored to ensure that interventions reach the target beneficiaries on time.
4. Various interventions proposed would be integrated with the district plan and targets for each identified district would be fixed.
5. Constant monitoring and concurrent evaluation for assessing the impact of the interventions for a result oriented approach by the implementing agencies.

Major Components of NFSM

1. National Food Security Mission – Rice (NFSM-Rice)
2. National Food Security Mission – Wheat (NFSM-Wheat)
3. National Food Security Mission – Pulses (NFSM-Pulses)

Total financial implications for the NFSM will be Rs.4882.48 crores during the XI Plan (2007-08 – 2011-12). Beneficiary farmers will contribute 50% of the cost of the activities / work to be taken up at their / individual farm holdings. Beneficiaries can choose to draw loans from the Banks, in which case subsidy amount prescribed for a particular component for which the loan availed will be released to the Banks. The implementation of the NFSM would result in increasing the production of rice by 10 million tonnes, wheat by 8 million tones and pulses by 2 million tones by 2011-12. It would also create additional employment opportunities.

States covered under NFSM

Total 136 districts of 14 States (AP, Assam, Bihar, Chhattisgarh, Gujarat, Jharkhand, Karnataka, Kerala, MP, Maharashtra, Orissa, Tamil Nadu, U.P. and West Bengal) will be covered under NFSM-Rice. Total 141 districts of 9 States (Punjab, Haryana, UP, Bihar, Rajasthan, MP, Gujarat, Maharashtra and West Bengal) will be covered under NFSM-Wheat. Total 171 districts of 14 States (AP, Bihar, Chhattisgarh, Gujarat, Karnataka, MP, Maharashtra, Orissa, Rajasthan, Tamil Nadu, Punjab, Haryana, UP and West Bengal) will be covered under NFSM-Pulses. Twenty million hectares of rice, 13 million hectares of wheat and 4.5 million hectares of pulses are included in these districts that roughly constitute 50% of cropped area for wheat and rice. For pulses, an additional 20% cropped area would be created. Panchayati Raj Institutions will be actively involved in the selection of beneficiary and identification of priority areas for the implementation of Mission interventions; and implementation of local initiatives in the identified districts.

(Sources:http://www.indg.in/agriculture/rural-employment-schemes/nfsm-operational guidelines.pdf, http://nfsm.gov.in/ and http://www.indg.in/agriculture/rural-employment-schemes/nfsm-operationalguidelines.pdf)

F. Technology Mission for Development of Horticulture in North Eastern Region including Sikkim

For integrated development of horticulture in a mission, mode to foster rapid growth/prosperity and to improve livelihood opportunities in the North Eastern region including Sikkim, a centrally sponsored schemes on Technology Mission, was approved by EFC (Expenditure Finance Committee) and CCEA (Cabinet Committee On Economic Affairs) has been launched from 2001-02. It is a Central Sector Scheme. The mission is based on the "end-to-end approach taking into account the entire gamut of horticulture development, which all backward and forward linkages, in a holistic manner. Considering the potential of horticulture for socio-economic development of Jammu &

Kashmir, Himachal Pradesh and Uttranchal, which are contiguous hilly states, Government of India have decided to extend the implementation of the Technology Mission to these states from 2003-04.

Objectives

The objectives of the Mission are to:

1. Establish convergence and synergy among numerous ongoing governmental programme in the field of horticulture development to achieve horizontal and vertical integration of these programmes.
2. Ensure adequate, appropriate, timely and concurrent attention to all the links in the production, post-harvest and consumption chain.
3. Maximise economic, ecological and social benefits from the existing investment and infrastructure created for horticulture development.
4. Promote ecologically sustainable intensification, economically desirable diversification and skilled employment.
5. Generate value addition, promote the development and dissemination of eco-technologies based on the blending of the traditional wisdom and technology with frontier knowledge such as biotechnology, information technology and space technology; and to provide the missing links in ongoing horticulture development projects.

Salient Features

The Technology Mission has four Mini Missions:

1. **Mini Mission-I (Technology Development /Research):** It aims to provide technical support by way of providing information on practices, nucleus planting material and skill up gradation for the adoption of technology. It will have a major link for the inflow of improved technologies. Mini Mission-I is coordinated and implemented by ICAR (Indian Council of Agricultural Research)
2. **Mini Mission-II (Production Enhancement):** This mini-mission primarily aims at increasing the quantum of

production and productivity of the horticulture produce in the region. The major activity in this mission would be increasing production through area expansion under various horticultural crops having linkages with other missions. Mini Mission-II is coordinated by DAC (Department of Agriculture & Cooperation, New Delhi) and implemented by the Agriculture /Horticulture Departments of these states.

3. **Mini Mission-III (Post –Harvest Management, Marketing & Export):** This mini-mission aims to create infrastructural facilities for post-harvest management, marketing and export. It is coordinated by DAC and implemented by NHB (National Horticulture Board), DMI (Directorate of Marketing Intelligence), NAFED (National Agriculture Cooperative Marketing Federation), APEDA (Agriculture And Processed Food Products Export Development Authority).
4. **Mini Mission-IV (Processing):** This mini-mission is coordinated and implemented by MFPI (Ministry of Food Processing Industries). Programmes which will be taken up by MFPI, are (a) Promotion of new units (b) Up gradation and modernization of existing units (c) Research & Development (d) Market Promotion (e) Human Resource Development.

(Source: http://webmani.nic.in/techmission/TechnologyMission.htm, http://india.gov.in/sectors/agriculture/tech_mission.php http://agro.indiamart.com/agro-programme-schemes/)

G. Integrated Scheme of Oilseeds, Pulses, Oil Palm and Maize

In order to provide flexibility to the States in implementation based on regionally differentiated approach, to promote crop diversification and to provide focused approach to the programmes, the schemes of Oilseeds Production Programme, Oil Palm Development Programme, National Pulses Development Project and Accelerated Maize Development Programme of Ninth Plan have been merged into one Centrally Sponsored Integrated Scheme of Oilseeds, Pulses, Oil Palm and Maize (IPOPOM) - External website that opens in a new window during the 10th Five Year Plan which is being implemented with effect from 1st April, 2004. The scheme is being implemented by 14 major growing

States for oilseeds and pulses and 15 States for Maize and in 10 States for oil palm.

Special features

1. Flexibility to the States to utilize the funds for the scheme/crop of their choice.
2. Annual action plan to be formulated by the State Governments for consideration and approval of the Government of India.
3. Flexibility to the States for introducing innovative measures or any special component to the extent of 10 per cent of financial allocation.
4. Involvement of the private sector by the State Governments for the implementation of the programme with a financial cap of 15 per cent.
5. Flexibility for inter-component diversion of funds up to 20 per cent for non-seed components only and
6. Diversion of funds from seed components to non-seed components with the prior approval of the Department of Agriculture and Cooperation.

Implementation of oilseeds production programme helped in increasing the production of oilseeds from 108.30 lakh tones in 1985-86 to 281.57 lakh tonnes during 2008-09 (IV Adv. Est.). The pulses production in the country increased from 128.60 lakh in 1989-90 to 146.62 (IV Adv. Est.) lakh tonnes in 2008-09. The area under Oil palm increased from 8,585 ha. at the end of 1992-93 to 26,178 ha. in 2008-09. The actual production of Fresh Fruit Bunches (FFBs) during 2008-09 is 355,480.36 MTs yielding around 59,007.40 Metric tonnes of Crude Palm Oil (CPO). The production of maize increased from 88.94 lakh tones in 1994-95 to 192.87 lakh tonnes in 2008-09 (IV Adv. Estimates).

(Source: http://india.gov.in/sectors/agriculture/index.php)

8.11 SUMMARY

For the development of agriculture, a number of programmes were launched in India. Some of the important programmes are Intensive Agricultural District Programme (IADP), High Yielding Varieties Programme (HYVP), Institute Village Linkage Programme

(IVLP), Watershed Development Programme, National Agricultural Technology Programme (NATP), National Agricultural Innovation Project (NAIP), Agricultural Technology Information Center (ATIC) and Agricultural Technology Management Agency (ATMA). These programmes contribute a lot to the development of agriculture in India.

8.12 KEYWORDS

- **Intensive Agricultural District Programme (IADP):** It was launched in the country from kharif, 1960. Initially, this was started with 7 districts. The immediate goal was to achieve rapid increases in agricultural production through a concentration of financial, technical, extension and administrative resources.
- **High Yielding Varieties Programme (HYVP):** The HYVP was launched in Kharif 1966-67. The sole objective was to increase the total food production by utilizing high yielding seeds of selected crops.
- **Institute Village Linkage Programme (IVLP):** The programme was initiated on a pilot basis in 1995. One of the objectives is to introduce technological interventions with an emphasis on stability and sustainability along with productivity and profitability taking into account environmental issues in well endowed and small production systems.
- **Watershed Development Programme:** Drought Prone Areas Programmes (DPAP), Desert Development Programme (DDP) and Integrated Wastelands Development Programme (IWDP) were implemented to check the diminishing productivity of wasteland and loss of natural resources. All these programmes were brought under the Guidelines for Watershed Development with effect from 1st April.1995. Again from 1st April 2003, IWDP, DDP and DPAP are implemented under Harywali programmes.
- **National Agricultural Technology Programme (NATP):** National Agricultural Technology Programme was conceived as a pilot project and was launched in November 1998. The overall objective of NATP was to revitalize the agricultural technology generation, assessment, refinement and dissemination systems.

- **National Agricultural Innovation Project (NAIP):** The project was started in July 2006. It is for facilitating the accelerated and sustainable transformation of agriculture in support of poverty alleviation and income generation through technological innovations by the public research organizations in partnership with farmer's group, the private sector, the civil society organizations and other stakeholders.
- **Agricultural Technology Information Center (ATIC):** Agricultural Technology Information Centre (ATIC) has been conceived and put into practice since 1998-99 under National Agricultural Technology Project (NATP) to realise the needs of the farmers irrespective of their locations and farming practices.
- **Agricultural Technology Management Agency (ATMA):** The institutional mechanism in the form of Agricultural Technology Management Agency (ATMA) at district level was pilot tested under Innovations in Technology Dissemination (ITD) component of National Agricultural Technology Project (NATP) in seven states and 28 districts of the country from 1998 to 2004.

8.13 CHECK YOUR PROGRESS

1. What are the main objectives of the Intensive Agricultural District Programme (IADP)?
2. State the salient features of High Yielding Varieties Programme (HYVP).
3. Why the Institute Village Linkage Programme was initiated?
4. Narrate the objectives of Watershed Development Programme.
5. Explain the objectives of National Agricultural Technology Programme?
6. Describe the National Agricultural Innovation Project (NAIP), its objectives and salient features.
7. Explain the salient features of Agricultural Technology Information Center (ATIC).
8. State the objectives and salient features of the Agricultural Technology Management Agency (ATMA).

CHAPTER 9

Social Justice and Poverty Alleviation Programme

9.0 OBJECTIVES

This chapter helps the students to understand important social justice and poverty eradication programme undertaken in India after independence. After completion of the unit, students will be able to:

- Describe the Integrated Rural Development Programme (IRDP), its objectives and salient features.
- State the Swarnjayanti Gram Swarozgar Yojana (SGSY), its objectives and salient features.
- Mention the Prime Ministers' Rozgar Yojana (PMRY), its objectives and salient features.
- Explain the Integrated Tribal Development Agency (ITDA), its objectives and salient features.

9.1 INTRODUCTION

Poverty as a phenomenon has existed since the beginning of known history. But as centuries rolled by and population increased, it began to appear on a mass scale. This focused attention for the first time on poverty as a social, as distinct from an individual problem. By the time India gained its independence, many countries, mostly in the West, had already overcome the problem of mass poverty by the application of new and progressively expanding scientific and technological knowledge. But in India, not only was the access to this knowledge limited, but its utilization had also lagged far behind. Mass poverty was, therefore, a serious social problem. Mahatma Gandhi had consistently projected poverty as a major social problem which required a concerted social response for eradication. After independence, therefore, alleviation of poverty was set up as a prime objective.

9.2 INTEGRATED RURAL DEVELOPMENT PROGRAMME (IRDP)

The programme was started in 1978-79. Initially, it covered 2300 selected blocks in the country and later it was extended to all the 5011 blocks with effect from 2 October 1980. It was the single largest anti-poverty programme of the country at that time. Different agencies implementing various programmes like the Small Farmers Development Agency, Drought Prone Area Programme, and Desert Development Programme etc. were merged under the programme. A new institution called as District Rural Development Agency (DRDA) was created to implement IRDP.

Objectives

It aims at providing income generating assets and employment opportunities to the rural poor to enable them to rise above the poverty line once and forever. The IRDP, in effect, seeks to redistribute assets and employment opportunities in favour of the rural poor.

Salient Features

1. It was a poverty eradication programme.
2. The IRDPs target group consisted of the poorest of the rural poor-small and marginal farmers, agricultural and non-agricultural labourers, rural artisans and craftsman, SC and ST families who live below the poverty line.
3. It employed a cluster approach to select villages for implementing various components of the programme. It followed the principle of the poorest of the poor first (antyodaya). The cluster approach ensured that the supporting infrastructure is either already available in the villages or can be made available at a relatively low cost. The package approach assured the beneficiary full benefits between various inputs and services.

4. IRDP beneficiaries are assisted through viable bankable projects which are financed party by subsidy and partly by bank loans. For economic activities, different rates of subsidies were provided to the target group.
5. The beneficiaries could select a project suited to his background, skills and personal preferences from a shelf of some sixty- one scheme in the fields of agriculture (5), irrigation (8), animal husbandry (9), village industries (29), tertiary sector (8) and others (2)
6. Creation of DRDA as an autonomous body at the district level to implement IRDP.
7. Under IRDP, a Community Development Block has been accepted as the unit for planning and implementation.
8. The IRDP provided training to both beneficiaries and functionaries at all levels.

Achievements

1. Around 40 per cent of the people had crossed the income level of Rs.3,500/- and around 55 per cent to 90 per cent had experienced some increase in their incomes during the Sixth Five Year Plan.
2. The financial and physical targets have been achieved during the seventh Five Year Plan.
3. During the Seventh Five Year Plan, the coverage of secondary and tertiary sectors had shown an increasing trend.
4. In the coverage of women beneficiaries, some states had crossed the target of 30 per cent and had done better than other states during the Seventh Five Year Plan.

9.3 SWARNJAYANTI GRAM SWAROZGAR YOJANA (SGSY)

Programme for self-employment of the poor has been an important component of the anti-poverty programmes implemented through government initiatives in the rural areas in India. The Swarnjayanti Gram Swarozgar Yojana (SGSY) is the major on-going programme for the self-employment of rural poor at present. The programme was started with effect from 01.04.1999 after review and restructuring of erstwhile Integrated Rural Development Programme (IRDP) and allied programmes, namely, Training of Rural Youth for Self Employment (TRYSEM), Development of Women and Children in Rural Areas (DWCRA), Supply of Tool kits in Rural Areas (SITRA) and Ganga Kalyan Yojana (GKY), besides Million Wells Scheme (MWS). The earlier programmes are no more in operation with the launching of the SGSY.

Objective

The basic objective of the SGSY is to bring the assisted poor families (Swarozgaris) above the Poverty Line by providing them income generating assets through a mix of bank credit and governmental subsidy. The programme aims at establishing a large number of micro-enterprises in rural areas based on the ability of the poor and potential of each area. The brief details of the programme are indicated in the following paragraphs.

Salient Features

1. Emphasis on the mobilization of rural poor to enable them to organize into Self Help Group.
2. Families below the poverty line (BPL) in rural areas constitute the target group of the SGSY. Within the target group, special safeguards have been provided to vulnerable sections, by way of reserving 50% benefits for SCs/STs, 40% for women and 3% for disabled persons.
3. Assistance under the SGSY, to individual Swarozgaris or Self Help Groups, is given in the form of subsidy by the government and credit by the banks. It is a credit-cum-subsidy scheme where credit is a critical component and subsidy is only an enabling element.
4. Participatory approach in selection of key activities: Each Block may select about 10 key activities, but the focus should be on 4-5 Key Activities based on local resources, occupational skills of the people and availability of markets so that the Swarozgaris can draw sustainable incomes from their investments.
5. Project approach for each key activity.
6. Emphasis on development of activity clusters to ensure proper forward and backward Linkages.

7. Strengthening of groups through Revolving Fund Assistance (RFA)
8. Training of beneficiaries in Group processes and skill development – an integral part of the project.
9. Marketing support with an emphasis on market research, upgradation/diversification of products, packaging, creation of market facilities, etc.
10. Provision for development of infrastructure to provide a missing critical link. 20% fund (in the case of NE State 25%) is earmarked for infrastructure development.
11. The active role of NGOs in the formation and capacity building of SHGs.
12. Focus on Vulnerable Groups, i.e. SC, ST, Women and Disabled
13. 15% fund earmarked for Special Projects to ensure a time-bound programme for bringing a specific number of BPL families above the poverty line.
    a) An SHG may consist of 10-20 persons belonging to families below the Poverty Line, and a person should not be a member of more than one group. In the case of minor irrigation schemes, disabled persons, and in difficult areas, i.e. hills, deserts and sparsely populated areas, the number of persons in a group may range from 5-20. However, if necessary 20% and in exceptional cases up to 30% of the members in a group may be from APL (marginally above the poverty line and residing continuously with BPL families) if agreed to by BPL members of the group. Efforts have to be made to involve women members in each SHG. 50% of Self-Help Groups in each block should be exclusively for women. Group activities are to be given preference. Majority of the funding should be for Self-Help Groups.
    b) The SGSY adopts a Project approach for each Key Activity. Project Reports are to be prepared in respect of each identified key activity. The Banks and other financial institutions have to be closely associated and involved in preparing these Project Reports, so as to avoid delay in sanctioning of loans and to ensure the adequacy of

financing. Selection of the activities has to be done with the approval of the Panchayat Samitis at the Block level and District Rural Development Agency/ Zilla Parishad at the District level. These Key Activities should preferably be taken up in Activity clusters so that the backward and forward linkages can be effectively established and economies of large scale production can be reaped. It is desired that a major share of the assistance to be provided under the SGSY should be for activity clusters.)

Achievements

1. On an average each year (since inception up to 2005-06) 66.86 per cent of the available fund was utilised and it was in increasing trends.
2. Regarding utilization of subsidy, 67.67% was utilized till 2005-06.
3. With respect to SHG since inception up to 2004-05, near about 19 lakhs SHGs were formed.
4. Total 2.4 lakhs SHGs (12.90 %) out of total SHGs formed till 2005-06 were able to take economic activities.
5. Awareness among people is increasing to form SHG under SGSY.
6. Different NGOs are also coming out to mobilise poor under this scheme.

9.4 PRIME MINISTERS' ROZGAR YOJANA (PMRY)

Prime Minister of India, announced a new scheme the Prime Ministers' Rozgar Yojana (PMRY) on 15th August 1993. The scheme was launched on the auspicious day of 2nd October 1993.

Objective

The main objective of the PMRY scheme was to provide easy subsidized financial assistance to educated unemployed youth for starting their own enterprises in manufacturing, business and service and trade sectors.

Salient Features

1. This is a centrally sponsored scheme
2. Parameters of PMRY:
   a) **Age**: For all educated unemployed between the age group of 18-40 years, in general with a 10 years relaxation for SC/STs, ex-servicemen, physically handicapped and women.
   b) **Educational Qualification**: 8th passed. Preference will be given to those who have been trained for any trade in Government recognised/approved institutions for a duration of at least six months
   c) **Family income**: Neither the income of the beneficiary along with the spouse nor the income of parents of the beneficiaries shall exceed Rs.40000 pa
   d) **Residence**: Permanent resident of the area for at least 3 years.
   e) **Defaulter:** Should not be a defaulter to any nationalized bank / financial institution/cooperative bank. Further, a person already assisted under other subsidy linked government schemes would not be eligible under this scheme.
   f) **Activities covered:** All economically viable activities including agriculture and allied activities but excluding direct agricultural operations like raising a crop, purchase of manure etc.
   g) **Project cost**: Rs.1.00 lakh for the business sector. Rs. 2.00 lakhs for other activities. If two or more eligible persons join together in a partnership, project up to Rs.10.00 lakhs are covered.
   h) **Subsidy and Margin money**: Subsidy will be limited to 15% of the project cost subject to a ceiling of Rs.7,500/- per entrepreneur. Banks will be allowed to take margin money from the entrepreneur varying from 5% to 16.25% of the project costs as to make the total of the subsidy and the margin money equal to 20% of the project cost.
   i) **Collateral**: No collateral for project up to Rs.1 lakh. Exemption from the collateral in case of partnership project will also be limited to an amount of Rs.1 lakh per

person participating in the project.

j) **Rate of interest and repayment schedule:** Normal bank rate of interest shall be charged. Repayment schedule may range between 3 to 7 years after an initial moratorium as may be prescribed.

k) **Reservation:** Preference should be given to weaker sections, including women. The scheme envisages 22.5% reservation for SC/ST and 27% for other Backward Class (OBCs). In case, SC/ST/OBC candidates are not available; States/UTs Government will be competent to consider other categories of candidates under PMRY.

3. The implementation agency at the grass root level is District Industries Centre (DIC).

Achievements

Initially, the scheme was aimed at providing self-employment to one million educated unemployed youth in the country by setting up 7 lakh micro enterprises through inducting service and business ventures over a period of 2 ½ years. The scheme was a stupendous success and caught the imagination of the youth. Overwhelmed with the response and ever-increasing need, the Government has decided to make it a permanent scheme and framed modalities and guidelines for its successful implementation and to fulfil the purpose for which it is designed.

9.5 INTEGRATED TRIBAL DEVELOPMENT AGENCY (ITDA)

A special programme for the development of selected tribal areas was initiated in 1970-71. This is called the Tribal Areas Development Programme (TADP). Under this programme six pilot tribal development projects were sanctioned - one in Andhra Pradesh (Srikakulam), one in Bihar (Chaibasa), two in Madhya Pradesh (Dantewara and Konta) and two in Orissa (Gunupur and Baliguda) as a Central sector scheme. Two more programmes were sanctioned as part of the programme during the Fifth Plan. Each of the projects was implemented through a society called the Tribal Development Agency. A detailed and comprehensive review of the tribal peoples' problem was taken up on the eve of the Fifth Five Year Plan period, and instruments of Tribal Sub Plan (TSP) was developed. TSP was implemented from 1974-75, the first year of the Fifth Plan. The Tribal sub Plan areas were divided into 180 Integrated Tribal Development Projects for operational purpose. Since ITDP is operated as Agency model under the Registration of Societies Act, 1860 and the ITDPs is also known as ITD Agency (ITDA).

Objectives

The main objective of ITDA/ITDP is socio-economic development of tribal communities through income generating schemes allied with Infrastructure Development programmes and protection of the tribal communities against exploitation.

The long term objectives of Tribal Sub-Plan are:

1. to narrow the gap between the levels of development of tribal and other areas; and
2. to improve the quality of life of the tribal communities.

Salient Features

1. Recognises that there is no uniform solution to the variety of problems facing tribal regions and tribal communities; therefore, accept the uniqueness and formulate policies, programmes and schemes to suit each individual situation and especially for vulnerable sections like Primitive Tribal Groups (PTGs), bonded labourers, shifting cultivators, forest villagers, displaced persons, etc.
2. Priority was given to agriculture and allied sectors
3. Infrastructures like roads and rural electrification were linked with economic development.
4. Evolve appropriate frame for development with an emphasis on tribal people at the national and State level through Sub-Plan exercise,
5. Accord highest priority to protective measures for elimination of exploitation of tribal people.
6. Restructure the administrative and institutional set up to suit the local needs and aspirations.
7. Supplement State efforts substantially by the Union Government

through Special Central Assistance (SCA).

8. The ITDA project areas are generally contiguous areas of the size of a Tehsil or Block or more in which the ST population is 50% or more of the total. Due to the demographic profile of the tribal people in these regions, however, the ITDPs in Assam, Karnataka, Tamil Nadu, and West Bengal may be smaller or not contiguous.
9. The ITDPs / ITDAs is headed by Project Officers though they may be designated as Project Administrators or Project Directors.

Achievements

1. So far, 194 ITDPs / ITDAs have been delineated in the country.
2. In many states, tribal development corporations were established for providing marketing support.
3. Special programmes were taken up for the development of most backward groups among the tribal communities.
4. Restructured administrative and institutional set up in tribal areas to suit the local needs and aspirations.

9.6 SUMMARY

Poverty is a major problem in India's development. It creates injustice in our society. So the government gives emphasis on poverty eradication. For that purpose, different poverty eradication programmes are introduced in India. Some of the major programmes are Integrated Rural Development Programme (IRDP), Swarnjayanti Gram Swarozgar Yojana (SGSY), Prime Ministers' Rozgar Yojana (PMRY), and Integrated Tribal Development Agency (ITDA). By providing opportunities through these programmes, the government gives economic support and social justice to poor people.

9.7 KEYWORDS

- **Integrated Rural Development Programme (IRDP):** The programme was started in 1978-79. It aims at providing income generating assets and employment opportunities to the rural poor to enable them to rise above the poverty line once and forever.

- **Swarnjayanti Gram Swarozgar Yojana (SGSY):** The programme was started from 01.04.1999. The basic objective of the SGSY is to bring the assisted poor families (Swarozgaris) above the Poverty Line by providing them income generating assets through a mix of bank credit and governmental subsidy.
- **Prime Ministers' Rozgar Yojana (PMRY):** The scheme was launched on 2nd October 1993. The main objective of the scheme was to provide easy subsidized financial assistance to educated unemployed youth for starting their own enterprises in manufacturing, business and service and trade sectors.
- **Integrated Tribal Development Agency (ITDA):** A special programme for the development of selected tribal areas was initiated in 1970-71. This is called the Tribal Areas Development Programme (TADP). Each of the projects was implemented through a society called the Tribal Development Agency. The main objective of the programme is socio-economic development of tribal communities through income generating schemes allied with Infrastructure Development programmes and protection of the tribal communities against exploitation.
- **Self- Help Group (SHG):** A SHG is a group of about 10- 20 people from a homogeneous class, who come together for addressing their common problems.

9.8 CHECK YOUR PROGRESS

1. What were the objectives of the Integrated Rural Development Programme (IRDP)?
2. What were the salient features of the Integrated Rural Development Programme?
3. State the salient features of Swarnjayanti Gram Swarozgar Yojana.
4. In what ways Prime Ministers' Rozgar Yojana (PMRY) is unique in nature?
5. Explain the objectives of the Integrated Tribal Development Agency (ITDA).

CHAPTER 10

Women Development Programmes

10.0 OBJECTIVES

This unit will discuss some of the important programmes of women. The chapter is aimed at providing students with an idea of important women development programmes of India. After completion of the unit, students will be able to:

- Describe the Integrated Child Development Services Programme (ICDS), its objectives and salient features.
- State the programme of Development of Women and Children in Rural Areas (DWCRA), its objectives and salient features.
- Mention the Rashtriya Mahila Kosh (RMK), its objectives and salient features.
- Describe the Mahila Samridhi Yojana (MSY), its objectives and salient features.

10.1 INTRODUCTION

Women constitute a significant proportion of the population. They play an important role in our society. Their economic contributions are generally not recognised. Their status in society is also very poor. Therefore special cares have to be taken for their development. So, the government launched some programmes which are meant for women and children.

10.2 INTEGRATED CHILD DEVELOPMENT SERVICES PROGRAMME (ICDS)

Following the experience of implementing welfare schemes for preschool children in 1972, the Planning Commission constituted an Inter-Ministerial study Team to review the existing services for children. The study team was to suggest a plan of action which would meet the total needs of children, avoid duplication or overlapping of services and optimally utilize the existing administrative and organizational structure. In consonance with the recommendations of this study team and the National Policy for Children adopted in 1974, the Integrated Child Development Services (ICDS) scheme was launched in 1975-76 in 33 community development blocks on an experimental basis.

Objective

The ICDS programme is designed to facilitate and promote "total development" of the child by making available an integrated package of services comprising mutually reinforcing components of health, nutrition and preschool education. The emphasis is on the crucial prenatal phase and the period of early childhood that is 0-6 years. Specifically stated, the objectives of the ICDS programme are:

1. To improve the nutritional and health status of children in the age group 0-6 years.
2. To lay the foundation for proper psychological, physical and social development of the child.
3. To reduce the incidence of mortality, morbidity, malnutrition and school drop-out.
4. To achieve effective coordination of policy and implementation amongst various departments to promote child development.
5. To enhance the capability of the mother to look after the normal health and nutritional needs of the child through proper nutrition and health education.

Salient Features

Strategy

The objectives of ICDS are sought to be achieved by providing a package of services to children in the 0-6 year age group, to expectant and nursing mothers and to women between 15-45 years from the disadvantaged segments of society. The essential components of the package are:

1. Supplementary nutrition
2. Immunization
3. Health check-up
4. Referral services
5. Nutrition and health education
6. Non-formal preschool education.

The Anganwadi is the focal point for the delivery of services under ICDS programme. There are a hundred anganwadis in each rural or urban project, covering a population of about 1,00,000. In each tribal project, there are usually fifty anganwadis covering a population of about 35,000. For rural and tribal projects under ICDS programme, priority is given to areas predominantly inhabited by SC, ST, backwards areas, drought-prone areas, nutritionally deficient areas and areas poor in development of social services. In the case of urban projects, priority is given to slums.

Services

Supplementary nutrition is an important service of the ICDS programme. It is provided to children below six years of age and to expectant and nursing mothers from low-income groups. Supplementary nutrition is given for 300 days in a year and consists of nutritious food prepared from locally available food materials. Supplementary nutrition under the programme provides 300 calories and 10 gm of proteins to all children below six-year, 600 calories and 20 gm of proteins to severely malnourished children and 500 calories and 20 gm of proteins to expectant and nursing mothers.

Immunization against diphtheria, whooping cough, tetanus, poliomyelitis and tuberculosis is provided to children in the project areas.

The arrangement is also made for periodic health checkup of children below six years, expectant women and nursing mothers to provide for appropriate and timely care of children and antenatal and postnatal care of mothers.

The health and nutrition education component of the programme is aimed at all women between 15-45 years of age but focuses on expectant women and nursing mothers.

Non-formal preschool education is a crucial component of the package of services provided under the ICDS programme and caters to the developmental needs of children between 3-6 years of age. Anganwadi workers stimulate the physical, motor, social, emotional, language and cognitive development of children.

Additional thrust area

The Department of Women and Child Development has launched schemes for adolescent girls as part of the ICDS programme, comprising an additional thrust area of the programme. Girl to girl approach and Balika Mandal are two schemes under this thrust area.

Administrative structure

The ICDS programme at the field level is implemented by a team comprising the Child Development Project Officer (CDPO), supervisors, Anganwadi Workers (AWWs) and helpers.

Community participation

ICDS is development oriented, and its ultimate success depends to a large extent on the participation of the local community in the programme.

Training of functionaries

The National Institute of Public Cooperation and Child Development (NIPCCD), New Delhi is the apex body for the training of ICDS functionaries. Training of CDPOs is the direct responsibility of NIPCCD. Training of supervisors is conducted by about 20 training centres located all over the country. Training of Anganwadi Workers has been entrusted to voluntary organizations, Schools of Social Work and College of Home Science etc.

Achievements

1. ICDS has brought about a reduction in the incidence of protein-energy malnutrition.
2. Health and nutritional status have improved in the project area after the programme has been in operation for some years.
3. ICDS programme resulted in -

a) Decline in incidence of nutritional anaemia.
b) The decline in the incidence of vitamin A deficiency.
c) Improvement in the nutritional status of children (0-6) years, expectant and nursing mothers.
d) Increase in birth weight
e) The decrease in infant mortality rate.
f) The decrease in morbidity rate

10.3 DEVELOPMENT OF WOMEN AND CHILDREN IN RURAL AREAS (DWCRA)

DWCRA was launched in 1982-83 as a pilot project in 50 districts chosen on the criteria of high infant mortality rate and low female literacy. There has been a phased expansion since then, and in 1989-90, DWCRA was being implemented in 106 districts.

Objective

The basic objective of DWCRA is to provide rural women with productive income-generating assets and credit and enhance their skills. It seeks support to provide an effective organisational support structure so that the women can receive assistance in the production of goods and services more effectively.

Salient Feature

1. The target group of DWCRA was the families who had an annual income of less than Rs.4,800/-
2. In DWCRA, instead of families, a group of beneficiaries receives assistance.
3. The scheme promotes the formation of the group, each consisting of 15 to 20 women; it was expected that the women would come together for activities which were mutually beneficial.
4. The financial assistance which was available for a group as follows-
   a) Rs.15,000 in the form of a one time grant contributed in equal measure by the Govt. of India, State Government and UNICEF, which was used as -
      i) Working capital to procure raw materials, and for

marketing purposes.

ii) Honorarium to group organizer which was not to exceed Rs.50 per month for a period of one year

iii) Infrastructural support for income-generating activities.

iv) Childcare facilities.

b) Travelling allowance at the rate of Rs. 2,000/- per year for one year for the group organizers.

5. DWCRA also included supportive services like mother and child care, adult education, immunization etc. For these purposes, coordination is maintained with various other departments such as Education, Health and Family Welfare, and Women and Child Development.
6. The training was provided to the selected beneficiaries of DWCRA for taking up economic activities.

Achievements

1. In some states like West-Bengal, DWCRA had been fairly successful in aiding women to produce products of good quality.
2. In Punjab, it has been successful in providing markets for the products.
3. Groups were formed by poor women to get assistance through DWCRA.

10.4 RASHTRIYA MAHILA KOSH (RMK)

It has been felt for some time in India that the credit needs of poor women, particularly in the unorganised sector, have not been adequately addressed by the formal financial institutions in the country. The vast gap between demand for and supply of credit to this sector established the need for a National Credit Fund for Women or the Rashtriya Mahila Kosh (RMK). It was set up in March 1993 as an independent registered society by the Department of Women and Child Development in Government of India's Ministry of Human Resource Development with an initial corpus of Rs. 3,10,000,000. The Kosh is established not to replace the banking sector but to fill the gap between what the banking sector offers and what the poor need.

Objectives

1. To promote or undertake activities for the promotion of or to provide credit as an instrument of socio-economic change and development through the provision of a package of financial and social development services for the development of women.
2. To promote and support schemes for the improvement of facilities for credit for women:
   a) for the sustenance of their existing employment
   b) for the generation of further employment
   c) for asset creation
   d) for asset redemption and
   e) for tiding over consumption, social and contingent needs
3. To demonstrate and replicate participatory approaches in the organization of women's groups for effective utilization of credit resources leading to self-reliance.
4. To promote and support experiments in the voluntary and formal sector using innovative methodologies to reach poor women with credit and other social services.
5. To sensitize existing government delivery mechanisms and increase the visibility of poor women as a vital and viable clientele with conventional institutions.
6. To promote research, study, documentation and analysis, including the provision of fellowships and scholarships, credit and its management and successful experiences at various levels in order to promote replication and dissemination of successful credit extension and management methodologies.
7. To promote the federation and networking of women's organisations for shaping & exchange of experience and information and to develop skills in response management and social mobilization.
8. To promote and support the expansion of entrepreneurship skills among women.
9. To cooperate with and secure the cooperation of the Central Government, State Governments and Union Territory Administration, credit institutions, industrial and commercial

organisations and non-governmental, voluntary and other organisations and bodies in promoting the objects of the Kosh.

10. To accept subscriptions, grants, contributions, donations, loans, guarantees, gifts, bequests etc. on such terms and obligations not inconsistent with the aims and objects of the Kosh
11. To do all such lawful acts & things as may be necessary or conducive for furthering the objects of the Kosh.

Salient Feature

1. RMK has three main roles:
   a) **Wholesaling Role:** it acts as a wholesaling apex organisation for channelising funds from government and donors to retailing intermediate microfinance organisations (IMOs).
   b) **Market Development Role:** It develops the supply side of the microfinance market by offering institution building support to new and existing-but-inexperienced IMOs by structures of incentives, transfers of technology, training of staff and other non-financial services.
   c) **Advocacy Role:** RMK acts as an advocate or agent for influencing the development and micro-finance policy and creating a more enabling policy and legal environment for the spread of micro-finance activities in India. Being a creation and a representative of the government, RMK has a particular advantage in this area.
2. There shall be no discrimination on the ground of religion, community, caste or class, creed or race in carrying out the aims and objects of the Kosh.
3. All the incomes, earnings, movable and immovable properties of the Kosh shall be solely utilized and applied towards the promotion of its aims and objects only.
4. The Kosh will seek to enable women to achieve economic independence.
5. While the provision of credit to cover composite needs is essential, such credit will be linked mainly to production and economic activity.
6. RMK creates an environment to facilitate and support further

innovation and experimentation for designing suitable delivery mechanisms to reach poor women.

7. Education of credit management will be integrated with the provision of credit, along with literacy and skill training for individual women, leadership training among groups for self-management, etc.
8. Accessibility of credit to poor women will be improved in terms of physical distance, simplification of procedures, the flexibility of measures for loans and recovery and other measures conducive to increase utilization, etc.
9. Provision of adequate, timely, regular flexible credit inputs matched to the individual needs of women allowing for the seasonality and diversity of poor women's work and occupations.
10. Promote and support grassroots level societies and organisations.
11. Establish a mechanism for dissemination of information and experience among agencies in the Government and non-government sectors in the area of credit for poor women.
12. To mobilize resources at several levels from governments, public and private donors and from other developmental agencies, both governmental and non-governmental.
13. Motivate voluntary organisations.
14. To coordinate with other credit and development agencies/ connected with the well being of women
15. To grant monetary and other assistance including loans/ guarantees to banks/ persons/organisations and associations, etc. who are engaged in the promotion and development activities for economic uplift of women.

Achievements

1. Total loan disbursed (up to May' 06) is Rs. 14,987.72 lakh
2. No of SHGs benefited (up to May'06) are 55,434 nos.
3. No. of women beneficiaries (up to May'06) is 54,9641 nos.

10.5 MAHILA SAMRIDHI YOJANA (MSY)

With the objective of providing economic security to the rural women and to encourage, the saving habit among them, the Mahila Samridhi Yojna was started on 2nd October 1993 by National Minorities Development And Finance Corporation, Ministry of Minority Affairs, Govt. of India (NMDFC).

Objective

1. Capacity building of minority women through increasing income-generating skills/activities;
2. Encouraging them to form SHGs and provide them microcredit support;
3. Setting up of production based activity suitable to minority women.

Salient Feature

1. Under this plan, the rural women of 18 years of above age can open their saving account in the rural post office of their own area with a minimum Rs. 4 or its multiplier.
2. On the amount not withdrawn for 1 year, 25% of the deposited amount is given to the depositor by the government in the form of encouragement amount.
3. Such accounts opened under the scheme are provided with 25% bonus with a maximum of Rs. 300 every year.
4. A group of 20 women of minority communities at any location are given training in any production/service activity, most suitable to them.
5. During the training, the group is formed into a Self Help Group practising thrift and credit.
6. MSY links micro-credit to the women after training. After the training, the group is provided credit, jointly or individually, for pursuing the activity of training
7. The scheme has been made broad-based to cover all the trades and activities practised by women.
8. The limit of micro-credit to each member of the Group is Rs.25000/- and the rate of interest to be paid by the women

beneficiaries have been reduced to 4%.

9. Maximum emphasis is given on the empowerment of minority women because they are the weakest link among the minorities.
10. Eligibility criteria for the beneficiaries:
    a) Women candidates belonging to minority communities with preference to widows and destitute.
    b) Preference to women already having some knowledge of the trade.
    c) Age 16-30 years
    d) Fulfil income criterion of below double the poverty line.
11. Stipend @ Rs. 250/- per month per candidate is deposited in the Bank account of the beneficiary or the SHG.
12. Beneficiaries are required to repay the loan over a period of 3 years after a moratorium of three months from the date of disbursement of the loan in monthly instalments.

Achievement

1. Up to 31 March 1997, 2.45 crore accounts were opened under this scheme with a total collection of Rs. 265.09 crore.
2. Numbers of groups are formed by minorities women under MSY
3. NGOs are also involved in this programme.

10.6 SUMMARY

In this unit, we discussed four women related programmes. Here we discussed why these programmes were launched and what the objectives of those programmes were to meet felt needs and cater to certain specific groups among the poor. We also discussed some of the achievements of those programmes.

10.7 KEYWORDS

- **Integrated Child Development Services Programme (ICDS):** Integrated Child Development Services (ICDS) scheme was launched in 1975-76 in 33 community development blocks on an experimental basis. The ICDS programme is designed to facilitate and promote "total development" of the child by making available an integrated package of services comprising mutually reinforcing components of health, nutrition and preschool education.

- **Development of Women and Children in Rural Areas (DWCRA):** DWCRA was launched in 1982-83 as a pilot project in 50 districts chosen on the criteria of high infant mortality rate and low female literacy. The basic objective of DWCRA is to provide rural women with productive income-generating assets and credit and enhance their skills.
- **Rashtriya Mahila Kosh (RMK):** It was set up in March 1993. Its initial corpus fund was Rs. 3,10,000,000. The Kosh is established not to replace the banking sector but to fill the gap between what the banking sector offers and what the poor need. The main objective is to promote or undertake activities for the promotion of or to provide credit as an instrument of socio-economic change and development through the provision of a package of financial and social development services for the development of women.
- **Mahila Samridhi Yojana (MSY):** It was started on 2nd October 1993 by National Minorities Development and Finance Corporation, Ministry of Minority Affairs, Govt. of India (NMDFC). Its main objective is to build the capacity of minority women through increasing income-generating skills/activities; encouraging them to form SHGs and provide them microcredit support; setting up of production based activity suitable to minority women.

10.8 CHECK YOUR PROGRESS

1. What are the basic objectives of ICDS?
2. Why DWCRA was introduced? What are the salient features of the programmes?
3. Write the importance of RMK?
4. Why MSY is launched? Who are the beneficiaries under this scheme?

CHAPTER 11

Reorganised Extension System - Training and Visit (T&V) System

11.0 OBJECTIVES

For disseminating technology to the farmers, an established extension system is necessary. In India first such system was CDP followed by NES. But due to some demerits, these systems were replaced by the Training and Visit System after reorganizing the existing system. This chapter is aimed at providing students with an idea of the Training and Visit system. After completion of the unit, students will be able to:

- Describe the key features of the Training and Visit (T&V) System
- State the linkage mechanism of the T&V system.
- Mention the objectives of a monthly workshop
- State the venue, frequency, and location of Monthly Workshop
- Mention the objectives of fortnightly training
- State the venue, frequency, and location of fortnightly training
- List the advantages of T&V sytem
- Mention the demerits of the T&V system.

11.1 INTRODUCTION

Training and Visit system was introduced in India in 1974 as a World Bank-funded project. It was initially pilot tested in Canal areas of Rajasthan and Chambal command areas of Madhya Pradesh. In Assam, it was introduced in 1977. Since this system reorganized and replaces NES in India, so it is also called a reorganized extension system. The system was developed by D. Benor and M. Baxter of World Bank. This chapter is adopted basically from

Benor and Baxter (1984).

11.2 KEY FEATURES OF THE TRAINING AND VISIT (T&V) SYSTEM

Benor and Baxter (1984) mentioned some key features of the T&V system, which are given below.

Professionalism

Extension staff must keep in close touch with relevant scientific developments and research so that he can advise the farmers in the right way. Extension workers must have the ability to identify production constraints in the field and to develop appropriate measures to counter them. This is achieved in T&V by fully and continuously training each extension worker to handle his particular responsibilities in a professional manner. In this way, credibility is built within the farming community. In addition, the requisite physical support for training and visit are also supplied.

Single Line of Command

The extension service is under a single line of technical and administrative command. All extension workers are responsible for administratively and technically to a unit within only one department. The department within which the service is located is solely accountable for the operation of the extension system, notwithstanding the required coordination and liaison with other organizations.

Concentration of Effort

Effective training and visit extension are based on a concentration of effort. Only by concentrating on the tasks at hand can the impact of extension become visible and can progress be sustained. The concentration of effort is a feature of all aspects of the system. All extension staff works only on agricultural extension. Staffs are not responsible for the supply of inputs, data collection, distribution of subsidies, processing of loans, or any other activity not directly related to the extension. All extension staff performs specific duties that complement and support the activities of staff at all other levels.

In training sessions, attention is concentrated on important major points. Similarly, extension-oriented research concentrated on key constraints faced by farmers to increase production and income. In sum, the concentration of effort means that the entire extension system is focused on bringing about the greater possible increase in the production and income of the farmers it service.

Time – Bound Work

Messages and skills must be taught to farmers in a regular, timely fashion, so that they will make the best use of the resources at their command. The VEW visit his farmers regularly on a fixed day (usually, but not necessarily, once each fortnight). All other extension staff makes timely and regular visits to the field, as required, to fulfil their job responsibilities. Recommendations for a specific area and for particular farming conditions for each two-fortnight period are discussed and learned by Subject Matter Specialists (SMSs) at regular monthly workshops. The recommendations are then presented to VEWs and Agriculture Extension Officers (AEOs) at the next two fortnightly training sessions. That means entire activities are time bound.

Field and Farmer Orientation

To serve farmers effectively, an extension service is in contact with them. Moreover, contact is on a regular basis, on a schedule known to farmers, and with a large number of farmers representing all major farming and socio-economic strata. The farmers served by a VEW are divided into groups; each group is visited on a fixed day once every two weeks by the VEW. All other extension workers, including SMSs, also spend a large part of their time in farmers' fields, generally on regularly scheduled visits. Researchers and trainers, as well as District Extension Officers and other senior staff, visit the field often and regularly to understand the problems faced by farmers (and by extension workers).

Regular and Continuous Training

Regular and continuous training is conducted under the T&V system. Regular and continuous training of extension staff is required both to teach and discuss with them, the specific production recommendations required by farmers for the coming fortnights and to upgrade and update their professional skills. Moreover, the basic training sessions (fortnightly training and monthly workshops) are a key means of bringing actual farmers' problems to the attention of researchers. It identifies research findings which have immediate relevance to farmers. It also develops production recommendations that fit specific local conditions. Without regular training, extension workers have very little of use to say to farmers.

Linkages with Research

The effective extension depends on close linkages with research. Linkages are two-way. Problems faced by farmers that cannot be resolved by extension workers are passed on to researchers for either an immediate solution or investigation. During seasonal and monthly workshops and joint field trips, extension and research staff formulates production recommendations considering the local situation of farmers. Research's awareness of and reaction to actual farm conditions is increased through responding to problems that have been put forward by extension workers, through the training of extension staff, and through field visits. This heightened awareness and taking account of local conditions has the beneficial effect of helping to orient some of the research attention to the important practical matter of farmers' production conditions and constraints.

11.3 LINKAGES OF T&V SYSTEM

Agricultural extension and research are mutually dependent. The extension requires the findings of research to teaching to farmers, as well as the support of research in solving farmers' problems. Without research's involvement, it is unlikely that extension will be able to teach the significantly improved practices (including new varieties, crops, and cropping patterns) that lead to the marked increase in productivity required for rapid, sustained agricultural growth. Similarly, research requires extension's guidance on problems that farmers face and on new issues that become apparent from field exposure and on which research attention should be focused on.

The dynamic, regular contact of extension workers with farmers under the training and visit system of extension makes effective linkages between researches. Consequently, to support training and visit extension, the linkages between extension and research are strengthened by a number of systematic procedures that encourage interaction between extension and research staff.

The most formal of the procedures facilitating extension/research interaction are joint extension/research committees and workshops where production recommendations are made, applied research and farm trial priorities and programs are established and evaluated. Such committees and workshops provide a framework for extension/research interaction, but effective linkages depend at least equally, if not more so, on a number of less formal measures. These include informal contacts between extension and research staff; exposure to one another during training programs when extension staffs are trained by research; collaboration in field testing and farm trials; and visits of extension staff to research stations and of research staff to farmers' fields. Some systematic and less formal means of linkage are reviewed below.

Formulation of Production Recommendations and Research Proposals

The formulation of both production recommendations and research proposals is a two-way process. Recommendations are based on the findings of the research and on actual field and production conditions as reported by extension staff and farmers and in light of the field experience of researchers. To help ensure that recommendations benefit from the input of both extension and research and, consequently, are relevant to farmers, they are established through a series of meetings of different groups, each of which includes representatives of research and extension and representative farmers. These groups usually include a State Technical Committee, seasonal zonal workshops, and monthly workshops.

Monthly Workshops

The frequency, activities, and composition of the monthly workshop make them one of the most important forms of extension/

research linkage. Monthly workshops serve mainly to train Subject Matter Specialists (SMSs), but they also play a critical role in the formulation of production recommendations, in the planning of farm trials, and in the analysis and interpretation of the results of the trials. The two-day multidisciplinary monthly workshops are attended by SMSs, Sub-divisional, District, and Zonal Extension Officers, as well as resource persons (or "trainers") who, generally come from research station of State Agricultural Universities.

Seasonal Zonal Workshop

The evaluation and programming of research and extension activities at a zonal level- a common agro-ecological zone, which usually comprises the area of several monthly workshops—are the responsibility of the seasonal zonal workshop. The workshop is normally organised by the Director of Research in collaboration with the Director of Extension and comprises both senior research staff and district and zonal extension staff, including Subject Matter Specialists. The main functions of the Zonal workshop (which meets before each season) are to review for the zone as a whole:

1. Proposed production recommendations for major crops in the light of research findings, field experience and the results of farm trials;
2. research priorities and research proposals;
3. plans for results of farm trials; and
4. plans for applied research activities, including verification trials at a number of locations. In the same manner that the seasonal zonal workshop takes account of state-wide priorities and adapts these to the agricultural production realities and priorities of the zone, so will monthly workshops adapt the findings and recommendations of the zonal workshop to local conditions.

State Technical Committee

The State Technical Committee provides guidance and direction to all research and extension activities in the state. The Committee meets before each season under the leadership of the Secretary of Agriculture, and its member includes a senior staff of research organizations and the Department of Agriculture. Through both the review of material from seasonal zonal workshops and independent initiative, it is able to coordinate and guide the work of research and extension on a state-wide basis. The State Technical Committee reviews and revises, as necessary, research plans (including guidelines for farm trials), objectives, and results. It establishes the general concerns of the extension service by approving sets of general zonal recommendations.

Research Involvement in the Training of Extension Staff

The Department of Agriculture is responsible for most of the training of extension staff, but an important role in training is played by research. Consequently, training courses can have a secondary role in encouraging professional contact between extension and research. While research staffs are often the trainers on short courses for extension staff, the most frequent and regular involvement of research in the training of extension staff comes through monthly workshops. All Subject Matter Specialists and Sub-divisional and District Extension Officers attend monthly workshops. The for monthly workshops resource persons may be anybody with experience in a particular field, but the main training responsibility falls to research staff.

Other Forms of Linkage

Field visits are an important means of extension / research contact. Research staff makes frequent field trips to review specific field problems raised by extension staff, understand general field conditions, and farm trials, and to assess farmer's reactions to production recommendations. Extension staffs encourage these visits by inviting research staff to accompany them. The field extension staff (especially SMSs) are encouraged often to visit the research stations to review research activities and findings in their particular areas of interest and relevance and, generally, to update their technical knowledge. Extension and research staff makes joint field trips to review the progress of farm and other trials. Finally, extension and research staff also has informal contacts deriving from areas of individual interest and participation in joint workshops and courses.

11.4 MONTHLY WORKSHOPS OF T&V

Objectives

The main objective of monthly workshops is to train subject Matter Specialists, particularly in the production recommendations that extension workers will teach farmers over a four-week period that usually starts some two or three weeks after the workshop (that is, the fortnight following the first fortnightly training session after the workshop).

The workshop is to cover six basic activities:

1. Review the rate of adoption of recommended practices by farmers and of problems regarding the adoption of recommended practices that have been brought to the attention of SMSs by extension workers and farmers or noted by SMSs or research workers during their own Field Visits.
2. Note difficulties faced by SMSs in presenting and explaining recommendations to extension workers during fortnightly training sessions.
3. Formulate and discuss recommended practices for major crops for the coming two fortnights, and sometimes for a longer period, if necessary; select for each recommendation, a few impact points on which extension workers should focus farmers' attention.
4. Review the climatic, input, and marketing situation of the area that may affect the adoption of recommendations, and ensure that recommendations take account of such conditions.
5. In practical and field sessions, train SMSs to carry out recommended practices themselves (by field demonstration and practice), and to present them effectively to extension workers in fortnightly training sessions; make field visits to review topical field situations and to develop SMSs' diagnostic skills.
6. Discuss the progress and results of farm trails that have been carried out by SMSs and other extension staff under their guidance.

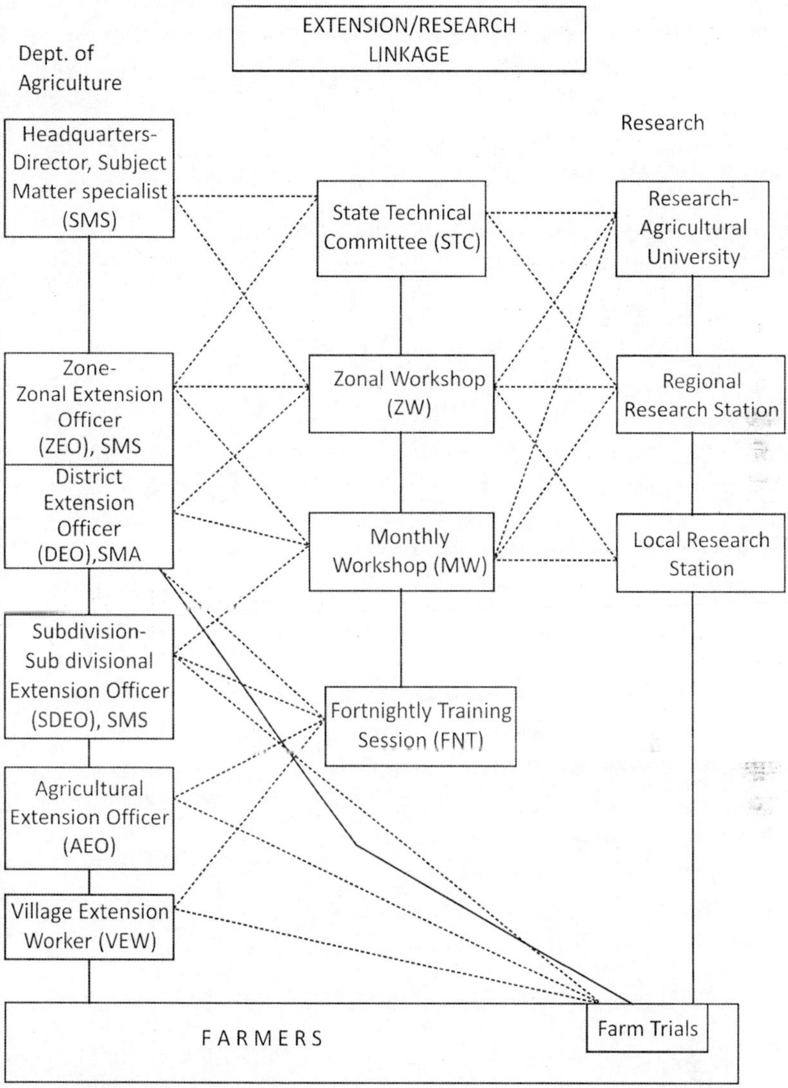

= Control

= Participation (only regular participation indicated)

(Fig. adopted from Benor and Baxter, (1984)

Two other important functions of monthly workshops are to provide a forum for extension and research to become familiar with each other's work and priorities, and for extension and research to learn from each other's experience through informal individual and group discussions – the learning that takes place through such discussions is as important as the formal learning of recommendations and solutions to farmers' problems.)

The venue, Frequency and Location of Monthly Workshops

Monthly workshops should be held at a research station that is conveniently located in the area from which participants are drawn. If a suitable research station is not available, an agricultural university or seed farm of the Department of Agriculture with appropriate facilities may be used. It is held on a fixed day of every month. Two full days are required for the workshop.

Participants of Monthly Workshops

Participants are both from the extension service and from universities and research agencies. Participating extension staffs are SMSs at the subdivision and district level and the Zonal, District, and Sub-divisional Extension Officers (ZEO, DEO, SDEO). The workshop coordinator is the senior participating officer of the Department of Agriculture - the zonal or district officer, as the case may be. The workshop coordinator is responsible for the overall effective planning of the workshop. The main trainers (or "resource persons") are researchers from agricultural universities and research stations who are thoroughly conversant with local crops and major crops in the area.

11.5 FORTNIGHTLY TRAINING/MEETINGS OF T&V

All village extension workers (VEWs) and Agricultural Extension Officers (AEOs) participate in one full day of training each fortnight, the "fortnightly training session." Fortnightly training is the chief means of continuously upgrading and updating the professional skills of extension workers and infusing them with confidence to meet farmers.

Fortnightly training sessions have two main objectives: One objective is to present specific recommended practices—in a series of key impact points - for the coming fortnight to the VEWs and AEOs for them to teach farmers of their groups. Extension workers should also be advised during training how to adjust these recommended practices to take account of specific local conditions. A second objective is that the training sessions should act as a link between field-level extension staff and research, via Subject Matter Specialists (SMSs).

At fortnightly training sessions, VEWs and AEOs report field problems and conditions that should be solved at the training session and taken into account in formulating recommended practices for the coming fortnight; problems that cannot be satisfactorily explained or solved answered by SMSs are taken to research staffs at the next monthly workshop, or earlier if circumstances warrant.

An important feature of fortnightly training is that representatives of local input supply and marketing agencies are present for part of relevant sessions. Extension workers report on the current input supply situation in their areas of jurisdiction and the likely short- and medium-term input requirements on the basis of the forthcoming production recommendations. Extension staffs are in turn advised of the availability of inputs, alternative materials, supply points, and market trends. Recommendations will be adjusted, as necessary, to incorporate this information, which extension workers will also discuss with farmers.

Location, Duration and Frequency of Fortnightly Training

Fortnightly training should be held at research stations, departmental farms, or on farmers' fields, depending on the facilities available and those required for a particular session. Only in rare cases should training be held in a classroom. VEWs and AEOs must learn and practice the skills involved in recommended messages because they have to teach the messages with confidence to farmers. Therefore adequate land must be available at the training location for practical fieldwork. Materials and equipment needed for teaching should be brought to the training site for each session if they are not available locally. The training location should be decided by the Subdivisional Extension Officer (SDEO), Training Officer, and SMSs involved. The location may be changed for particular sessions, depending on the requirements of the topics to be covered. Whatever location is to be used, however, it must have good facilities for practical work. All participants at a training session should be told where the next session will take place.

A fortnightly training session will last one full day, starting as early as convenient for participants to reach the training location and ending in time for VEWs to be able to get home.

Fortnightly training is held every two 'weeks, not on the basis of twice a calendar month. Training is always held on the same day of the fortnight for a training group. Where there is more than one training group in a subdivision, the training days of each group must be different, since the trainers will be the same for all the groups in a subdivision.

Participants of Fortnightly Training

The number of participants should not be more than thirty VEWs and AEOs. It is always useful also to invite a few farmers to participate in the training. Sub-divisional SMSs are the principal trainers. District or State-level SMSs (and other extension staff) and research scientists should participate occasionally. Where a sub-division has more than thirty VEWs and AEOs, they should be divided into groups of fifteen to thirty on the basis of the location of their areas of operation. The SDEO is the organizer and leader of all fortnightly training sessions held in his subdivision.

11.6 MERITS OF T&V SYSTEM

1. Principles underlying the system are basically simple and can be widely applied in a different situation.
2. It involves the systematic application of well-known management principles.
3. The financial cost of the system to farmers is also very small.
4. The system is designed to achieve results rapidly.
5. The extension staff under the T&V system is fully trained to handle one's particular responsibility in a professional manner.
6. The extension staffs are under a single line of command.
7. All extension staff are working on agriculture production only
8. There is an effective span of control for supervision

9. The activities of extension agents are time bound
10. There have a field and farmers orientation in case of extension staff
11. There is an effective linkage between extension and research
12. The extension staff are continuously trained on agricultural production recommendation

11.7 DEMERITS OF T&V SYSTEM

1. The programme is staff intensive and had been found to suffer in places where adequate staffs are not in position.
2. Except for crop production, almost all other enterprises of the farmers have remained untouched by the programme
3. Information for the farmers in many cases was of a routine type
4. In training, the emphasis was on technology and very little on extension methods
5. Emphasis was on personal contact of the extension agent with a few selected farmers
6. Existing village leaders and village institutes have been neglected
7. Lack of adequate interaction between contact farmers and other farmers.

11.8 SUMMARY

Our extension system was reorganized through the Training and Visit system. It has some advantages over CDP and NES due to some salient features of the system. Its effort is concentrated on agriculture. Though it has some advantages, it has some disadvantages too.

11.9 KEYWORDS

- **Monthly Workshop:** It is held at a monthly interval. The main objective is to train subject Matter Specialists, particularly in the production recommendations that extension workers will teach to farmers over a four-week period that usually starts some two or three weeks after the workshop.

- **Fortnightly Training:** It is held at the fortnightly interval. It is the chief means of continuously upgrading and updating the professional skills of extension workers and infusing them with confidence to meet farmers.

11.10 CHECK YOUR PROGRESS

1. Briefly discuss the key features of the Training and Visit (T&V) System.
2. Why the linkage mechanism is so important in the T&V system?
3. State the objectives of the monthly workshop of the T&V system?
4. Why fortnightly training is conducted?
5. What are the advantages of the T&V system?
6. Mention the demerits of the T&V system.

CHAPTER 12

New Trends in Extension

12.0 OBJECTIVES

To fulfil the increasing need for farmers, some new extension trends are taking place in our extension system. This chapter is aimed at providing students with an idea of a few such new trends in the extension system. After completion of the unit, students will be able to:

- Define private extension and privatization of extension
- Differentiate between private extension and privatization.
- Mention the stakeholders of private extension and privatization
- Describe the reason for the privatization of extension
- Mention some privatization approaches of extension.
- Define contract farming
- List the advantages of contract farming
- Mention the limitation of contract farming
- Define cyber extension
- List the information to be provided through cyber extension
- Mention the advantages of cyber extension.
- State the limitations of cyber extension
- Describe the necessity of Farmers led extension
- Differentiate between production led and farmers led extension
- State the importance of market-led extension
- Differentiate between production led and market-led extension
- Mention the principles and characteristics of Farmers Filed School.

12.1 INTRODUCTION

Now our agriculture is aiming at commercialization and farmer's orientation is changing. Our farmers now- a -days do not depend only on the public extension system. They are collecting information from various sources. At the same time, to get the maximum benefit, some farmers started to practice contract farming. In this context, numbers of players, as well as the use of information technologies in extension, are increasing day by day. Hence, new trends in the extension are coming up.

12.2 PRIVATE EXTENSION AND PRIVATIZATION

The definition of Agricultural Extension varies from a simple transfer of information to facilitating the process of total human development. The services are mainly funded and delivered by the government. But there are private players who also fund and/or deliver extension services. This process of funding and delivering the extension services by private individual or organization is called Private Extension (Chandra Shekara, 2001). Bloome (1993) indicated that private sector extension involves personnel in the private sector that delivers advisory services in the area of agriculture and is seen as an alternative to a public extension. Van den Ban and Hawkins (1996) state that in private sector extension, farmers are expected to share the responsibility for the service and pay all or part of the cost. Schwartz (1994) notes that private sector extension is not a stand-alone activity but will be provided where three conditions hold as follows:

1. Purchased inputs must be necessary to achieve desired production results
2. This purchased inputs must be cost-effective relative to output prices
3. There should be a fairly high degree of competition between input suppliers for the same market share.

On the other hand, privatization is the act of reducing the role of government or increasing the role of the private sector in an activity or in the ownership of assets. Very often Private Extension and Privatization are viewed similarly. Private Extension is solely the act of private individuals or organizations, whereas the decision of privatization solely rests with the government and implemented in liaison with Private Extension Service Provider (PESP). Hence both are different (Chandra Shekara, 2001).

B. Stake Holders in Private Extension/Privatization

According to Chandra Shekara (2001) in the process of privatization, the public extension is always a part. In private extension, players may be agricultural consultants, agricultural consultancy firms, progressive farmers, farmer's organization/cooperatives, non-governmental organization (NGO's), Krishi Vigyan Kendras, agri-business companies, input dealers, newspapers, agricultural magazines, private television channels, private sector banks, internet and donor agencies etc. Private and public extensions are the two sides of the same coin called agricultural extension. Both aim at serving the ultimate client farmer in different ways. Hence, they are the co-partners in the process of development of farmer. The private extension is not a substitute for a public extension.

C. Reason for Privatization of Extension Services

Extension service is a challenging task, with over 100 million people living in more than half a million villages. For providing these services, with the role of extension personnel is most crucial in the developmental process. Right now, information plays a key role in taking many decisions in bringing desirable change in society. For this matter, information technology is helping in a fantastic way. It is interesting that computer-aided extension has the potential to transform the agricultural scenario by providing farmers with the right kind of models and alternatives in the complex climate and market system of the country. For pursuing the farmer's complicated problems, it can no longer be dealt with effectively from a centralized and bureaucratic entity. Therefore, the time has come to infuse change wherever possible to the private sector for support but not for total substitution (Chandra Shekara, 2001). However, some of the most important reasons he mentioned for privatization are given below:

1. **Fiscal crisis:** Many less developed country's governments have found it difficult to make adequate resources available for extension. Financial pressures have, in turn, led to the search

for ways of reduction in public sector costs, e.g. privatization of extension services.

2. **Poor performance:** Public extension system has certain weakness like manpower deficit, lack of technical knowledge of extension workers etc.
3. **Changing contexts and opportunities:** Due to the improved transport network, NGOs are reaching to remote villages, mass media as radio and television are also available in the villages. Government agencies are not among the top primary sources of information for many farmers in India at present.
4. **Trained and untrained extension worker:** Extension workers in public extension services are not well trained to tackle the problems of rural people.
5. **Experience shows that diversity is the only way to address changing conditions and various categories of users**. Since users are more likely to seek advice from more competent sources, public vs private extension is likely to result in which only the best sources are retained.

The private sector is now engaged in many of the activities that are being done by the public sector extension. Privatization of extension assumes great significance. It is found that private enterprises are far more efficient than governmental agencies in delivering goods and services. Farmers do not hesitate to pay for valuable information, full proof services and delivery mechanism (Chandra Shekara, 2001).

D. Consequences of Privatization/Private Extension

According to Chandra Shekara (2001) following are the consequence of privatization/private extension:

1. The commercial interest of private extension services may also jeopardise the efforts presently being made by public research and extension systems towards achieving eco-friendly and sustainable agriculture.
2. Educational goal played by public extension agencies at present may be lost in case extension services are privatized.
3. It will increase regional imbalances.

E. Privatization Approaches

According to Chandra Shekara (2001) following are some approaches of privatization/ private extension, which could be tried in India.

1. **Share copping system:** The extension worker provides advisory service and inputs. Farmer uses his land and labour. Extension worker shares the crop with the farmer for profit. Hired labour and costs are shared
2. **Extension contract system:** Agricultural consultant/firm will provide advisory and inputs to individual farmer or group. The cost of input is recovered after the harvest.
3. **Village extension contract system**: An agricultural advisory committee consisting of representatives of farmers at village level hire consultancy. Consultant work for the village as per the requirement of the village. Here it is a group approach.
4. **Contract farming**: The Agri-business firm provides all inputs and technology. It also supervises the production process. As per the MOU, the farmer has to sell his product as per quality specified, to the firm only at a premium price.
5. **Public extension through private delivery:** Agricultural consultancy firms are graded and certified by a government agency. Depending on capacity, extension services are awarded to competitive bidders at different levels is state, district, block/village etc. The service cost is shared between the government and clients.

12.3 CONTRACT FARMING

A. Definition

Contract farming is agricultural production carried out according to an agreement between a buyer and farmers, which establishes conditions for the production and marketing of a farm product or products. Typically, the farmer agrees to provide established quantities of a specific agricultural product, meeting the quality standards and delivery schedule set by the purchaser. In turn, the buyer commits to purchase the product, often at a pre-determined price. In some cases the buyer also commits to support production through, for example, supplying farm inputs, land preparation, providing technical advice and arranging transport of produce to the buyer's premises. Another term often used to refer to contract farming operations is "out-grower schemes", whereby farmers are linked with a large farm or processing plant which supports production planning, input supply, extension advice and transport. Contract farming is used for a wide variety of agricultural products.

Contract farming refers to contractual arrangements between farmers and companies whether oral or written, specifying one or more conditions of production and/or marketing of an agricultural product (Ramesh, 1999)

Singh (2005) defined contract farming as a system for the production and supply of agricultural and horticultural produce by farmers/ primary producers under advance contracts, the essence of such arrangements being a commitment to provide an agricultural commodity of a type, at a specified time, price and in specified quantity to a known buyer. Contract farming may be extended to other fields like animal, fishery, forestry production etc.

B. The rationale for Contract Farming

Contract farming is one of the different governance mechanisms for transactions in agrifood chains. The use of contracts (either formal or informal) has become attractive to many agricultural producers worldwide because of benefits such as the assured market and access to support services. It is also a system of interest to buyers who are looking for assured supplies of produce for sale or for processing. Processors are among the most important users of contracts, as they wish to assure full utilisation of their plant processing capacity. A key feature of contract farming is that it facilitates backwards and forward market linkages that are the cornerstone of market-led, commercial agriculture.

C. Advantages of Contract Farming

Contract farming has some advantages both to the producers and to the contract farming companies. Important advantages of contract farming are presented in the following pages (Saravanan and Gowda, 2003).

1. **Economic security to farmers/producers:** contract farming system provides an assured price for agricultural produce to the farmers and reduces the risk and uncertainty in the commodity price fluctuation. Growers have ensured a stable and sustained market for their produce.
2. **Effective technology transfer:** Contract farming provides effective technology transfer to farmers. Case study on tomato contract farming in Punjab reveals that it provides new and better farming skills and better soil management practices.
3. **Timely input supply:** For successful contract farming, ensuring quality inputs at the appropriate time is crucial. In contract farming, corporates give farmers access to inputs like high yielding seeds, new plant varieties, better quality fertilizers and pesticides. Contract farming in Punjab, Karnataka, and Tamil Nadu revealed that the concerned companies are supplying the needed seeds and seedlings to the farmers. This, in turn, reduces the need for operational capital of the farmers.
4. **Infrastructure facilities:** Corporate in contract farming will develop efficient storage and transport facilities, cutting down on wastage. Besides, the corporate sector will add value to the farm produce by setting up processing units (Sandhu, 1998)
5. **Efficient and effective national agricultural production system:** Corporatisation of agriculture through contract farming may have many long term benefits; better allocative efficiency; higher private investment; an increase in output, income and exports; and a higher multiplier effect leading to the creation of wealth in rural India. Further, increased productivity and production leads to reduced cost of production as well as the expansion of value-added product market at domestic and international level.

D. Limitations of Contract Farming

Some limitations of contract farming are as follows (Mandal and Ray, 2007):

1. **Create regional and socio-economic imbalance:** Small and marginal farmers may not be able to meet the huge expenditure on inputs as recommended by corporates in contract farming.

In fact, the eligibility criteria for participation in contract farming projects/schemes like irrigated land, fertile land, land near the main road, the literacy level of the farmers etc. are themselves discriminatory in terms of who can be a contract grower. Considering India's vast rainfed areas, contract farming may create regional and socio-economic imbalance.

2. **Insecurity problem:** From the experience of contract farming in Punjab, contract farmers complained about problems of high cost of transportation, delay in payment, the vulnerability of crop failure and deduction in the price for poor quality (Singh, 2001). Contract farming has created a new set of middlemen who keep a margin and pay a lower price to the producer.
3. **Unsustainable farm practices:** Commercial interest of contract farming will jeopardize achieving and practising sustainable farming. Repeated cultivation of the same crop without rotation can lead to a variety of soil and pest hazards which have been reported in many situations in the contract farming of tomatoes (David and Ken, 1990). Contract farming in Punjab also revealed that corporate are recommending and using higher doses of pesticides and fertilizers.
4. **Food security of the nation may be at stake:** Corporate will concentrate only on high-value crops such as horticultural crops and other cash crops. Food grain production and processing may not attract private investment. Increased emergence of corporate in contract farming may disturb the food security of the nation.

12.4 CYBER EXTENSION

A. Concept and Definition

Lack of feedback mechanism in the Research - Extension Linkages is identified as one of the weaknesses in existing Extension Systems. Communication is the most critical element in Research-Extension-Farmer-Marketing loop. Now media and ICTs offer strong potential to improve this mechanism (Sharma, N.D.).

The cyber extension is an agricultural information exchange mechanism over cyberspace, the imaginary space behind the interconnected computer networks through telecommunication means. It utilizes the power of networks, computer communications and interactive multimedia to facilitate information sharing mechanism (Wijekoon, 2003). Cyber Extension is the extension over Cyber Space.

Cyber Space is the imaginary or Virtual space of computers connected with each other on Networks, across the globe. These computers can access information in the form of Text, Graphics, audio, video and animation files. Software tools on networks provide facilities to interactively access the information from connected servers. The cyberspace thus can be defined as the imaginary space behind the interconnected telecommunications and computer networks, the virtual world. The weak linkages among extension, research, marketing network and farmers limits the effectiveness of research and extension to contribute to agricultural development. The Government of India has identified this problem and is addressing it through national programmes. The erstwhile emphasis on the usage of vernacular press, radio and television for reaching to the farmers is being augmented with the use of state-of-the-art communication technologies such as Internet and satellite communication. Under the new initiative of NATP, adequate attention is being paid to provide ICT connectivity down to the Block level. This connectivity will facilitate two-way communication among all the stakeholders in the Research-Extension- Farmers- Marketing loop. Apart from core Information and Communication Technology (ICT) connectivity, other forms of audio and visual communication like Satellite Communication (SATCOM) are also being promoted on a project basis (Sharma[1] nd)

According to Sharma[2] (nd), access to information and improved communication is a crucial requirement for sustainable agricultural development. He observed that modern communication technologies - when applied to conditions in rural areas - can help to improve communication, increase active participation and further the dissemination of information and sharing of knowledge and skills. He believes that cyber extension will be the major form of technology dissemination in the near future, allowing for the fact that the rural population still has difficulty in accessing crucial information in order to make timely decisions.

B. Information Provided through Cyber Extension

The cyber extension can provide a large amount of information to farmers. Some of those, as mentioned by Sharma (nd) are given below:

1. **Weather:** Daily information of maximum and minimum temperature, day length, direction and speed of the wind, rainfall, relative humidity and weather forecasting.
2. **Alert:** Information regarding the type of disaster, a sudden change in weather, an outbreak of diseases and insects etc.
3. **Insurance:** Detail information about insurance of farmer, his crop, animal and agricultural assets like tractors, implements and tools etc.
4. **General awareness:** Information about vaccination, cleanliness, health, family planning and nutrition.
5. **Rural finance:** Information about microfinance and subsidy etc.
6. **Education:** Detail information about farmers training and educational knowledge of his children about the professional and non-professional institution.
7. **Animal Science:** The detail regarding the local animal and well-known diseases, better breeds, balanced feed, shed management, health etc.

C. Advantages of Cyber Extension

1. Information can be provided quickly to farmers.
2. Information is demand driven.
3. Numbers of information can be disseminated at a time.
4. Farmers can get the solution instantly.
5. Provides facility to access market etc.

D. Limitation of Cyber Extension

1. Lack of reliable telecom infrastructure in rural areas.
2. Erratic or no power supply.

3. Lack of ICT trained manpower (willing to serve) in rural areas.
4. Lack of content (locally relevant and in local language).
5. Rural people can not afford cyber extension due to low purchasing power etc.

12.5 FARMER LED EXTENSION

Farmer led extension in agriculture is the process through which individuals or groups within a given locality discover or develop and apply improved ways of managing the available resources, building on and expanding the boundaries of their indigenous knowledge. All farmer-led extension is not of a technical nature but rather are socio-economic and institutional extensions. The concept of farmers extension is applied to agriculture technology process that aims to improve rural livelihood for sustainable development while ensuring inter-institutional and farmer learning.

Over the years, farmers also selected several varieties that had higher productivity and better quality. Farmers have also developed new and low-cost techniques to preserve, process and package various farm products both for increased shelf life and better market opportunities. Despite these, the innovations made by farmers have not received the recognition, which they deserve. Also, the property rights on the innovations made by the farmers have often been ignored. In order to promote development as farmers led skills as well as protect their rights, it is necessary that we recognize and further promote these innovations. It is also desirable to blend the existing traditional wisdom with modern scientific knowledge for ensuring sustainable agriculture. Farmers extension processes are inexpensive easily accessible, locally appropriate and already tested in real form practice. They are therefore more rapidly accepted by other farmers that are the results of formal research. Through informal trials with ideas from multiple sources, farmers make technology their over reality and often improve its efficiencies, effectiveness, productivity profitability, durability, marketability, sustainability etc. Farmers extension is also a way as life for poor farmers who are being challenged by the ever-changing environmental policy and market situation in the country. For them, the extension is not academic work or an extracurricular activity. Rather it is an inherent characteristic as those who are striving to make a living out of the difficult situation they are in. Almost every single farmer who is living in such challenging circumstance has to innovate in order to survive.

The Farmers Led Extension approach gives farmers the opportunity to share their experiences and practices through a method demo with fellow farmers in the area. It was noted that farmers who were successful in their farming venture had established credibility among their peers. These very same farmers are just waiting to be tapped to act extensionist in their barangay. In selecting the farmer extensionist, the primary consideration is - he should be an innovative farmer, active and hardworking, honest and credible, interested in learning, accepted and committed to the community, and most importantly interested in sharing his knowledge and skills Likewise, a farmer extensionist must have conducted a techno-demo trial and field day, preferably attended the FFS. He must also have the capacity and willingness to finance the cost of technology. Farmer led extension approaches have proliferated due to the dissatisfaction with results from traditional extension programmes and the contraction as funding for public extension. There are 5 types of farmers led extension; farmer to farmer extension farmer field schools, the problem census,/problem-solving approach; NGO government collaboration and others. The category of "other farmer-led extension approaches include a variety of program models that provide limited external assistance to farmers and allow farmers to manage to adopt and spread the innovation through their over efforts. Monitoring and evaluation are difficult in farmer-led extension programme as activities and targets cannot be pre-planned, activities vary between communities and farmers, and farmer extensionists are often not interested.

(http://bicol.da.gov.ph/News/2005news/2qtr05/fle.html)

Table 12.1: a Paradigm shift from production-led to farmer-led extension system (Kokate et al., 2009)

Components	Production-led	Farmers-led
Purpose/ Objective	Transfer of production	Capacity building (especially farmers extensionist), create para-professional technologies extension workers, creating or strengthening local institutions
Goal	Food self-sufficiency	Livelihood security including food, nutrition, employment to alleviate poverty, sustainability and conserving biodiversity
Approach	Top-down, commodity and	Participatory, bottom-up and demand driven supply driven
Actors	Mostly public institutions	Pluralistic with public, private, non-government and farmers organizations as a partner rather than competitors
Mode	Mostly interpersonal/ individual approach	Integration of clients oriented on-farm participatory/experiential learning methods supported by ICTs and media
Role of extension agents	Limited to delivery mode and feedback to the research system	Facilitation of learning, building overall capacity of farmers and encouraging farmers' experimentation
Linkages/ liaison	Research-Extension-Farmers	Research- Extension-Farmers Organizations (FIGs, CIGs, SHGs)
Emphasis	Information management, Production "Seed to Seed."	Knowledge management and sharing
Nature of technology	Input-intensive, crop-based and general recommendations as per agro-climatic zone, a fixed package of information	Knowledge-intensive, broad-based, farming system perspective, and blending with ITKs.

Components	Production-led	Farmers-led
Critical areas	Improvement, production and protection	Decision support system, integrated farming system approach, natural resource management, clients group formation and community empowerment
Critical inputs	Money and material	Access to Information, building human and social capital
Accountability	Mostly government	To farmers rather than donors

12.6 MARKET LED EXTENSION

The focus of extension agencies on production technologies yielded very good results, and hence, India becomes self-reliant on food production. Significantly, the extension system had played its role untiringly in the transfer of production technologies from lab to land, besides the agricultural scientists, farmers and marketing network. But the farmers at the individual level do not realize remunerative prices for their produce. Add to this; the Indian farmers have to face challenges of a global force that are affecting or are likely to affect Indian agriculture. This assumes greater significance in the light of the new international trading regime under WTA and the export opportunities being opened up. Therefore extension functionaries need to play a major role to build the capacity of the farmers to meet the emerging challenges and make the farmers to realize better prices to their farm produce. But, Market – led extension so far is a peripheral issue in the extension scenario. Hence the extension focus should extend from mere production to market-led extension on an end-to-end basis. The focus of the extension functionaries needs to be extended beyond production. Farmers should be sensitized on various aspects of quality, consumer's preference, market intelligence, processing and value addition and other marketing information. This will help the farming community to realize high returns for the produce, minimize the production costs, and improve the product value and marketability (MANAGE, 2008)

With the globalization of the market, farmers need to transform themselves from mere producers-sellers in the domestic market to producers cum sellers in a wider market sense to best realize the returns on their investments, risks and efforts. In order for this to be achieved, farmers need to know answers to questions like what to produce, when to produce, how much to produce, when and where to sell, at what price and in what form to sell their produce. Farmers have received most of the production technologies from the extension system. The extension system now needs to be oriented with knowledge and skills related to the market (Reddy and Chandrashekara, 2009)

Agriculture without economy is nothing. So the market linkage is a must for Agriculture. The market is a congregation of prospective buyers and sellers with a common motive of trading a particular commodity. The extension is the spreading/reaching out to the mass. Market-led Extension is the agriculture and economics coupled with extension is the perfect blend for reaching the doorsteps of the common man with the help of technology. Market-led Extension is the market ward orientation of agriculture through extension.

Basics of Market-Led Extension

- Market Analysis
- Market Intelligence
- Use of Technology

Aspects of Market-Led Extension

- Community Mobilization
- Forming CIGs
- Forward and Backward Linkages
- Improvement of the effectiveness of existing markets
- Improvement of efficiencies of marketing channels

(Source: http://www.authorstream.com/Presentation/nikesh_saye-739349-market-led-extension-122847298998928 1-9/)

Table 12.2: Paradigm Shift from Production-led Extension to Market Led Extension (Adopted from MANAGE, 2008)

Aspects	**Production-led extension**	**Market-led extension**
Purpose/ objective	Transfer of production technologies	Enabling farmers to get optimum returns out of the enterprise
Expected end results	Delivery of messages Adoption of a package of practices by most of the farmers	High returns
Farmers seen as	Progressive farmer High producer	Farmer as an entrepreneur "Agripreneur"
Focus	Production / yields "Seed to seed."	The whole process as an enterprise / High returns "Rupee to Rupee."
Technology	Fixed package recommended for an agro-climatic zone covering huge area irrespective of different farming situations	Diverse baskets of a package of practices suitable to local situations/ farming systems
Extensionists' interactions	Messages Training \ Motivating Recommendations	Joint analysis of the issues Varied choices for adoption Consultancy
Linkages/ liaison	Research-Extension-Farmer	Research-Extension-Farmer extended by market linkages
Extensionists' role	Limited to delivery mode and feedback to the research system	Enriched with market intelligence besides the TOT function Establishment of marketing and agro-processing linkages between farmer groups, markets and processors
Contact with farmers	Individual	Farmers' Interest Groups Commodity Interest Groups /SHG's
Maintenance of Records	Not much importance as the focus was on the production	Very important as agriculture viewed as an enterprise to understand the cost-benefit ratio and the profits generated

Aspects	Production-led extension	Market-led extension
Information Technology support	Emphasis on production technologies	Market intelligence including likely price trends, demand position, current prices, market practices, communication network, etc. besides production technologies

12.7 FARMER FIELD SCHOOL

The term "Farmer Fields School" came from the Indonesian expression Sekolah Lapangan. The Farmer Field School is a form of adult education, which evolved from the concept that farmers learn optimally from field observation and experimentation. In regular sessions from planting till harvest, groups of neighbouring farmers observe and discuss dynamics of the crop's ecosystem. In this cyclical learning process, farmers develop the expertise that enables them to make their own crop management decisions. Special group activities encourage learning from peers and strengthen communicative skills and group building.

Principles of the Farmer Field School Approach

Communication: Communications in extension have come to mean the marketing of information packages. Messages are crafted to focus on a particular aspect, put on flip charts, the mass media, or on posters that are developed in central offices. In addition, they may be disseminated to farmers via 'model' demonstration farms.

Education: Education is the most important aspect that an 'extension' program can do and the farmer is the most important person being educated. Within the educational approach, communication must take place at the field level, dealing with field issues in a dialogue with learners. The communication model cannot do this. However, it can be done within the context of farmer field schools. The farmer field school deals not only with the practice that farmers want to learn about but with farmers as farmers. Farmer field schools are conducted for the purpose of helping farmers to master and apply field management skills. The farmer implements his or her own decisions in his or her own field.

Problem-Posing/Problem-Solving: Within this form of training, problems are seen as challenges, not constraints. Farmer groups are taught numerous analytical methods. Problems are posed to groups in a graduated manner such that trainees can build confidence in their ability to identify and tackle any problem they might encounter in the field.

Field-based education: Education in the classroom can only mimic the natural world. Putting the classroom in the field allows the field to be the learning material and the farmer to be able to learn from real-life examples. Putting the classroom in the field means that the educator (extension worker) must come to terms with the farmer in the farmer's domain.

Principle not Packages: The Farmer Field Schools teaches several principles, bring out cause and effect relationships, principles help farmers discover and learn, principles help farmers learn to learn so that they can continue to learn. Packages have nothing to do with learning and do not encourage learning; in the long run, they are neither cost-effective nor effective at improving the quality of farmers management skills. Skilled farmers can optimise yields independently of others. Packaged approaches increase the dependence of farmers on central planners.

Training driven research: Research must be responsive to field needs. By and large, researchers have got it backwards. Research programs in agriculture drive the extension or education programme that the research should actually be serving. What farmers need to know to be able to operate sustainable, both environmentally and economically, should drive the research program. In the Farmer Field School approach, all research is based on training needs or is an adjunct of training. Farmers have become a part of the research network supporting educational programmes.

Characteristics of the Farmer Field School Approach

Farmers as Experts: Learning by doing is the training approach used. Farmers learn by carrying out for themselves the various activities related to the particular farming practice they want to study and learn about. This could be related to annual crops, livestock/fodder production, orchards or forest management. The key thing is that farmers conduct their own field studies. Their training is based on comparison studies (of different treatments) and field studies that they, not the extension/ research staff conduct. In so doing, they become experts on the particular practice they are investigating.

The Field is the Primary Learning Material: All learning is based in the field. The field is where the farmers learn. Working in small sub-groups, they collect data in the field, analyse the data, make action decisions based on their analyses of the data, and present their decisions to the other farmers in the farmer field school for further discussion, questioning, and refinement.

Extension Workers as Facilitators Not Teachers: The role of the extension worker is very much that of a facilitator rather than a conventional teacher. Once the farmer knows what they have to do, and what they can observe in the field, the extension worker takes a back seat role, only offering help and guidance when asked to do so. Presentations during meetings are the work of the farmers, not the extension worker, with the members of each working group assuming responsibility for presenting their findings in turn to their fellow farmers. The extension worker may take part in the subsequent discussion sessions but as a contributor, rather than a leader, in arriving at an agreed consensus on what action needs to be taken at that time.

The curriculum is Integrated: Crop husbandry, animal husbandry, horticulture, silviculture, are considered together with ecology, economics, sociology and education to form a holistic approach. Problems confronted in the field are the integrating principle.

The training follows the Seasonal Cycle: Training is related to the seasonal cycle of the practice being investigated. For annual crops, this would extend from land preparation to harvesting. For fodder production would include the dry season to evaluate the quantity and quality at a time of year when livestock feeds are commonly in short supply. For tree production and soil conservation measures as hedgerows and grass strips training would need to continue over several years for farmers to be able to see for themselves the full range of costs and benefits.

Regular Group Meetings: Farmers meet at regular intervals. For annual crops, such meetings may be every 1 or 2 weeks during the cropping season. For other farms/forestry management practices, the number of meetings depends on specific activities need to be done.

Learning materials are learner-generated: Farmers generate their own learning materials, from drawings of what they observe to the field trials themselves. These materials are always consistent with local conditions, are less expensive to develop, are controlled by the learners and thus can be discussed by the learners with others. Learners know the meaning of the materials because they have created the materials.

Group dynamics/team building: Training includes communication skill, problem-solving, leadership, and discussion methods. Farmers require these skills. Successful activities at the community level require that farmers can apply effective leadership skills and have the ability to communicate their findings to others.

12.8 SUMMARY

To serve the need of the farmer's new trends are coming up in extension. Some weaknesses of public extension and commercialisation of agriculture also lead to introduce private extension and privatization. With the development and expansion of telecommunication services, different organisations introduced cyber extension in rural areas. Commercial agriculture also initiates contract farming. Though new trends have some advantages, these are also not full proof.

12.9 KEYWORDS

- **Private extension:** The process of funding and delivering the extension services by private individual or organization is called Private Extension.
- **Privatization:** It is the act of reducing the role of government or increasing the role of the private sector in an activity or in the ownership of assets
- **Contract farming:** Contract farming is agricultural production carried out according to an agreement between a buyer and farmers, which establishes conditions for the production and

marketing of a farm product or products.

- **Cyber extension:** Cyber extension is an agricultural information exchange mechanism over cyberspace, the imaginary space behind the interconnected computer networks through telecommunication means.
- **Farmers led extension:** Here, experienced and interested farmers are acting as an extensionist.
- **Market-led extension:** here, extension service is provided based on market demand.
- **Farmers Field School**: It is an adult learning process.

12.10 CHECK YOUR PROGRESS

1. What is a private extension?
2. Differentiate between private extension and privatization.
3. Who ate the stakeholders of private extension?
4. Why privatization of extension is needed?
5. Define contract farming and highlight its advantages.
6. What is a cyber extension?
7. What type of information we can provide through a cyber extension?
8. Mention the advantages and limitations of cyber extension.
9. Why Farmers led extension is important in present-day context?
10. Differentiate between production led and farmers led extension?
11. State the importance of market-led extension?
12. In what way production led is different from the market-led extension?
13. Mention the principles and characteristics of Farmers Filed School.

CHAPTER 13

Emergence of Broad-Based Extension

13.0 OBJECTIVES

The broad-based extension (BBE) is also an approach of extension for increasing income of the farmers. This unit will help the students to know about the concept of BBE, its purpose and difficulties. More specifically, at the end of the unit, the students will be able to:

- Define broad-based extension
- State the purpose of BBE
- Mention the difficulties of BBE
- Give suggestion for implementation of BBE

13.1 INTRODUCTION

India is an agricultural country, and its economy is mainly based on agricultural production. So, the development of this country solely depends on agriculture. The T& V system of agricultural extension introduced during the 70s has contributed lots by increasing both production and productivity of the field crops. But it has proved less fruitful towards sustainable agriculture. At present, most of the farmers, irrespective of their holdings have felt the importance of the farming system, which not only concerns with agriculture but also many other enterprises such as horticulture, forestry, fishery, sericulture along with soil and water management practices. This system facilitates the optimum utilization of farm resources for higher income generation.

In India, about 70% of cultivable lands are under the rainfed condition, and farm holdings are characterized by infertile, flood-prone, drought-prone, waterlogged soil and irregular distribution of fertile normal land. Moreover, the ecology, social factor and marketing facilities also vary from place to place. Therefore, the farming system in India should be based upon complex interactions among different enterprises to minimize the risk in farming practices and thus to increase the total return. Realizing the importance of farming system during the mid-'80s the present agricultural planning shifts its interests from production orientation to farmer's income orientation.

13.2 DEFINITION

The idea of broadening the scope of agricultural extension on bringing a number of farm activities in addition to the crop production under the umbrella of agricultural extension is called a broad-based extension (Dayal, 1993).

As the BBE is a multidisciplinary approach; hence, the success in implementation and adoption will obviously depend on proper coordination among the concerned development departments along with active Government policies.

13.3 PURPOSE OF BEE

The purpose is of multi-directional, and it can be summarised as follows:

1. To improve the socio-economic condition of the farmers
2. To generate employment opportunities
3. To utilize the available farm resources properly
4. To maintain soil fertility & prevent soil erosion and to balance the existing ecosystem
5. To facilitate setting-up of different agro-based Industries
6. To overcome the risk related to the environmental hazards
7. To provide self-sufficiency to the farmers for various farm products.
8. To enhance coordination and better understanding among the different department to increase the total farm production
9. To enhance the dissemination of various technologies of different disciplines to the farmers
10. To increase farmers satisfaction and esthetic values
11. To put special attention to the farm women in various aspects

of the farm activity.

13.4 DIFFICULTIES IN IMPLEMENTING BBE

Lots of difficulties are related to the implementation of broad-based extension, which results in the adoption/acceptance of this system by limited states. The difficulties which have been felt are noted as follows:

1. Lack of coordination among different disciplines / departments
2. Financial constraints of the Govt. for implementing the proposed system.
3. Difficulties related to input supplies.
4. Lack of proper marketing and infrastructure facilities, mainly related to storage, processing and transportation
5. Lack of technical knowledge of the farmers.
6. Lack of interest of the farmers to adopt a new production strategy.
7. The poor economic condition of the farmers.
8. Inadequate credit facilities
9. Difficulties arising due to religion and other social values
10. Most of the farmers are not business minded, hence their production mainly confined with their own needs.

13.5 SUGGESTION FOR PROPER IMPLEMENTATION OF BBE

Dayal (1993) suggested the following point regarding successful implementation of BBE.

1. BBE would have to be implemented in phase covering land-based activities in the first phase and other activities such as fisheries and sericulture in the second phase.
2. Technology input in BBE should be synthesised on a zonal basis to offer a broad-based package for monthly workshop which should be essentially the responsibility of chief scientist of RARS.
3. Coordination mechanism needs to be established and developed at various levels.

4. Identification of expertise available in the line department and ensuring their participation in the zonal/monthly/fortnightly interface.
5. Continuous monitoring of the implementation of BBE at various levels, identifying constraints and providing necessary feedback to the research system is essential.
6. For wider coverage, efforts of NGOs and social action groups should be encouraged.

13.6 SUMMARY

On the basis of the purpose of BBE, it is clear that BBE would become a successful system to increase farm production and to augment the present production barriers. BBE, if implemented properly, will improve the present socio-economic status of the farmers. There are lots of difficulties associated with the implementation of BBE. In this regards, the suggestions made for proper implementation should be given more priority.

13.7 KEYWORDS

- **Broad-based extension:** The idea of broadening the scope of agricultural extension on bringing a number of farm activities in addition to the crop production under the umbrella of agricultural extension is called a broad-based extension.

13.8 CHECK YOUR PROGRESS

1. What do you mean by broad-based extension?
2. What is the purpose of broad-based extension?
3. What are the difficulties for the implementation of broad-based extensions?
4. Give some suggestion for proper implementation of the broad-based extension.

CHAPTER 14

Important Policies of Agriculture

14.0 OBJECTIVE

For the development of the agricultural situation of India recently two important policies are adopted by the Government. For the benefits of the students, these two policies are mentioned in this unit though these are not included in the syllabus. This unit will help the students aware of these policies.

14.1 POLICY FRAMEWORK FOR AGRICULTURAL EXTENSION

Rapid agricultural growth continues to be the key to poverty alleviation and overall economic development. Agriculture accounts for about one-fourth of the Gross Domestic Product and is the source of livelihood or nearly two-thirds of the population. The agriculture sector in India has been successful in keeping pace with the rising food demand of a growing population, expected to cross one billion. Food grains production more than quadrupled since the early 1950s from 51 million tons to over 209 million tons in 2000, while the population nearly tripled from 350 million to one billion during the same period.

The Green Revolution has been the cornerstone of India's agricultural achievement, transforming the country from one of food deficiency to self-sufficiency. While recognizing the impact of the Green Revolution in imparting dynamism to the agriculture sector, it must be recognized that the Green Revolution remained restricted to the well-endowed irrigated areas of the country. Of late, deceleration in production and of factor productivity growth in some of the major irrigated production systems, especially in the North and North-West regions, has been recorded. Potentially high production areas (Eastern and the Central States) are still lagging behind in productivity increases. Moreover, in the area of agricultural research, success has been restricted to selected crops. Even in this arena, a growing disparity between the actual and the potential yields points to a crucial gap between research and extension.

Public research and extension played a major role in bringing about the Green Revolution. In the post-Green Revolution era, however, extension faces important challenges in the areas of relevance, accountability and sustainability. The changing economic scenario in India and the need for appropriate agricultural technologies and agro-management practices to respond to food and nutritional security, poverty alleviation, diversifying market demands, export opportunities, and environmental concerns is posing new challenges to the technology dissemination systems. It is expected that future agricultural growth would largely accrue from improvements in productivity of diversified farming systems with regional specialisation and sustainable management of natural resources, especially land and water. Effective linkages of production systems with agro-processing and other value-added activities, including marketing, would play an increasingly important role in the diversification of agriculture.

It is becoming increasingly evident that public extension by itself can no longer respond to the multifarious demands of farming systems. There is a need for a reappraisal of the capacity of agricultural extension to address, effectively, contemporary and future needs of the farming community. Public funding for sustaining the vast extension infrastructure is also under considerable strain. Meanwhile, in response to market demand, the existing public extension network is inexorably being complimented, supplemented and being replaced by private extension. As the nature and scope of agricultural extension undergo fundamental changes, the outlook is for a whole new policy mix nurturing a plurality of institutions.

Changing Role of Agricultural Extension

The community development approach to extension

Public sector extension has undergone several changes since the early 1950s. Beginning with the Community Development Programme in 1952 through the National Extension Service in 1953, the focus of extension was on human and community development, but there has been a steady progression towards technology transfer, with the Intensive Agriculture District Programme started in 1961-62, followed by the Intensive Agriculture Area Programme in 1964-65, the High Yielding Varieties Programme 1966-67, the Farmers Training and Education Programme 1966-67 and the Small and Marginal Farmers Development Programme in 1969-70.

Transfer of technology approach through T & V

The most significant recent development was the introduction of the Training and Visit (T&V) extension management system, starting in the mid-1970s. T&V extension was well suited to the rapid dissemination of broad-based crop management practices for the high yielding wheat and rice varieties that were released since the mid-1960s. The T&V system profoundly influenced extension practices and registered impressive gains in irrigated areas, because of the similarity between the agro-ecological conditions where technologies were generated and where they were ultimately used, and the favourable socio-economic situations and developmental infrastructure for their wider uptake. Indeed, the T&V system played an important role in ushering in the Green Revolution.

Limitations of the T & V system

The focus of the T & V system being on disseminating Green Revolution technology for major cereal crops, extension activities have been largely carried out by State Departments of Agriculture (DOA). The other line departments, such as the Departments of Animal Husbandry (DAH), Horticulture (DOH), and Fisheries (DOF), have not been able to focus on extension due to lack of infrastructure, trained personnel and resources. The T&V system operated largely in the inter-personnel mode without planned and optimum utilisation of information support and with a low level of involvement of farmers. The "top-down" approach generated uniformity rather than specificity and lacked focus on location-specific needs of regions, disadvantaged areas, target groups enterprises etc. Individual and institutional issues under Human Resource Development, the training of researchers, subject matter specialists and extension functionaries and farmers had not been addressed adequately. The linkages between research-extension and farmer remained weak or non-existent. Media and information management largely remained in the public sector and characterized by centralized operations. Farmer-driven and farmer accountable feedback systems were not adequately developed.

Post-green revolution period

The transfer of T&V extension approach to rainfed farming areas where fundamentally different production systems predominate and more importantly, local conditions vary widely, resulted in serious limitations and failures. The system well suited to the rapid dissemination of pre-set agronomic practices for the high yielding wheat and rice varieties failed to respond to the more location-specific, risk-prone agriculture of the unirrigated tracts. Similarly, extending the system to programmes for natural resource management, sustainable agricultural practices such as integrated pest management, integrated nutrient management and to diversified agriculture such as high-value horticulture, livestock activities and fisheries did not meet with success. Nor could the T&V system adapt to the more holistic Farming Systems Approach towards which the new thrust of both research & extension had begun to focus.

Towards a farming systems approach

The extension approaches of the 1950s and 1960s centred around 'farmers' ignorance' as an explanation of non-adoption of agricultural technology and therefore the extension policies remained confined to "extension education" with the key activities related to "teaching". In the decade of the 1970s and 1980s, farm level constraints were considered to be the explanation of non-adoption. The key activities of the extension system were confined to 'input supply' for removal of such farm level constraints. The basic philosophy of these extension approaches centred on "technology transfer". By the early 1990s and the completion of the third National Agricultural Extension Project (NAEP), there was a growing recognition that the T&V extension approach needed to be overhauled in meeting the technology needs of farmers during the 21st century. First, it was recognised that extension should begin to broad base its programmes, by utilising a Farming Systems approach. For example, attention should be given to the needs of farmers in rainfed areas, and to diversifying extension programmes into livestock, horticulture, and other high-value commodities that would increase farm incomes. Secondly, to support and strengthen the Farming Systems approach, issues of financial sustainability, farmer participation in programme planning, and research-extension linkages, marketing and value addition would have to be concurrently addressed. Present-day agriculture is defined by key concepts of stability, sustainability, diversification and commercialization. There is a need for reorientation of the philosophy of extension from technology transfer mode to technology application.

Proposed Extension Policy Framework

In the context of meeting the holistic needs of increasing agricultural production, yet do so in a sustainable manner, agricultural extension has a crucial role to play. Reforms in the system envisage an extension service more broad-based and holistic in content and scope, thus beyond agricultural technology transfer. Its normal task of transferring and disseminating appropriate technologies and agronomic practices would not be sufficient. Extension agencies, services and workers will need to exercise a more proactive and participatory role, serve as knowledge/ information agents, initiating and facilitating mutually meaningful and equitable knowledge-based transactions among agricultural researchers, trainers and primary producers. All this needs to be done in an effective and cost-efficient manner.

Technology generation and its application will have to focus more strongly than before on the themes of optimization by producers of their available resources, sustainability, coping with diversity by adapting technology more specifically to agro-ecological or social circumstances aimed at creation of a policy environment that promotes profitable, productive and sustainable farming.

Reforms in agricultural extension already initiated and proposed to be undertaken on a wider scale are discussed under the following sub-heads:

- Institutional Restructuring
- Management Reforms
- Strengthening Research –Extension Linkages
- Capacity building & Skill Upgradation
- Empowerment of Farmers
- Mainstreaming of Women in Agriculture
- Use of Media & Information Technology
- Financial Sustainability
- Changing Role of Government

Policy Reforms

Farming systems approach

Policy reforms in Agricultural Extension envisage the replacement of the old single-discipline based, the commodity-oriented approach of the T & V system by the Farming Systems (FS) approach. The FS approach considers the farm, the farm household and off-farm activities in a holistic way to take care not only of farming but also aspects of nutrition, food security, sustainability, risk minimisation, income and employment generation which make up the multiple objectives of farm households. FS considers interdependencies of the components under the control of members of the household as well as how these components interact with the physical, biological and socio-economic factors not under the household's control. The FS approach emphasises that research and extension agendas should be determined by explicitly defined farmers' needs through an understanding of the existing farming systems rather than perceptions by research scientists or extension functionaries.

Multi-Agency Extension Service

For many years agricultural extension was considered the monopoly of the public sector. However, with the wide range of demands for agricultural technology in the changing scenario, there is growing recognition that public extension by itself cannot meet the specific needs of various regions and different classes of farmers. The new extension regime recognizes the role of a multi-agency dispensation comprising different strengths. Policy environment will promote private extension to operate in roles that complement, supplement, work in partnership and even substitute for a public extension. The three arms of the agricultural extension network are:

(a) Public extension services

1. State government line departments operated extension (Departments of Agriculture, Horticulture & Livestock development).
2. State agriculture universities based extension (Directorates of Extension, Krishi Vigyan Kendras (KVKs) and Krishi Gyan Kendras (KGKs).
3. ICAR extension (Zonal Research Stations/ Krishi Vigyan Kendras, Agriculture Technology Information Centres (ATICs), Institute Village Linkage Programme (IVLP) etc.)

(b) Private extension services

1. Community-Based Organization (Farmers' Organizations, Farmers' Cooperatives, Self Help Groups etc.)
2. Para Extension Workers (contact farmers, link farmers, *gopals, mitra kisans, mahila mitra kisans, etc.*)
3. Agri-Clinics & Agribusinesses
4. Input Suppliers/ Dealers (Pesticides, Seeds, Nutrients, Farm Implements, etc.)
5. Corporate Sector (Commercial Crops – tobacco, tea, coffee, oilseeds (sunflower), vegetables, Seeds, Farm Implements – tractors, threshers, sprinklers, drip irrigation, etc.)

(c) Mass media and information technology

1. Print Media – Vernacular Press
2. Radio, Television, Private Cable Channels, etc.
3. Electronic Connectivity through Computers, NICNET, Internet, V-SAT, etc.
4. Farm Information and Advisory Centres (FIACs)
5. Private Portals
6. Public & Private Information Shops

Public extension services

Despite the rise of the private sector in the provision of agro-services, such extension will gravitate towards selected regions, crops and sectors where gains are to be appropriated. Pure public goods, economically backward regions, small, marginal farmers and landless labourers will not attract the for-profit private sector. Public Extension will, therefore, continue to play a central role in technology dissemination. For example, the public extension should focus its efforts on those knowledge-based technologies that are central to farmers' concerns, and that will maintain the natural resource base. These are subject matter areas that are not likely to be taken by the private sector. Examples include dissemination of production management technologies that are specific to different crops and livestock systems; natural resource management technologies, such as soil and water management, integrated pest management, agroforestry and other technologies associated with sustainable development; and farming systems technologies, including farm management skills that will enable farmers to improve their efficiency, increase cropping intensities and to diversify into more high value commodities in conformity with marketing trends.

Promotion of farmer participatory approach

There is, therefore, need for a more farmer participatory approach in working out the system description, problem diagnosis, search for appropriate technology, designing the process of implementation, monitoring and evaluation, and feedback. The extension agent is no longer seen as the expert who has all the useful information and technical solutions; the indigenous technical knowledge of farmers and their ingenuity, individually and collectively, are recognized as a major source; and solution to local problems are to be developed in partnership between the extension agent and farmers. Extension workers, therefore, need new skills of negotiations, conflict resolution and mobilizing and nurturing community organizations.

Promotion of demand-driven and farmer-accountable extension

Under the T&V system, the technology dissemination regime was more supply-driven. Research and extension agendas were pre-set based on technologies for high-yielding varieties of wheat and rice. An important reason why research and extension organisations have not focused on farmer problems is due to the lack of an effective feedback system. The vast majority of small and marginal farmers in India, especially women, lack an effective voice in influencing, research and extension priorities. Under the new policy agenda, a demand-driven extension system will be created, by providing farmers with access to linkage mechanisms through which they would be provided with all relevant information/data to help them articulate their problems and needs with reference to their production & marketing plans. A key factor in improving these feedback systems is to organise farmers into functional groups, such as Self-Help Groups (SHGs), Farmer Interest Groups (FIGs), Commodity Associations (CAs), and/or other types of farmer organisations (FOs). These FOs can provide, an effective channel for both the dissemination of technology to a large number of small and marginal farmers and feedback to research and extension. Linkage mechanisms would also ensure meaningful farmer representation in the governing bodies of public and private extension services, farmer influence on decisions on the planning, implementation and monitoring of public extension at local, regional and national levels and farmer influence on the incentives of extension staff, including supervisors and subject matter specialists.

Thrust on marketing extension

Farmers have increasingly begun to perceive marketing rather than production as the major constraint to enhancing farm incomes. With a major thrust of extension agencies on production techniques, marketing extension so far has not received the attention it deserves. This assumes greater significance in the light of the new international trading regime under the WTO and the export opportunities being opened up. Public extension functionaries are presently ill-equipped to deal with marketing extension. The multi-agency extension service will need to address these issues through strengthening the capacity of the public agency, supporting the private sector in marketing extension and making extensive use of media and IT in information and technology dissemination. Marketing extension so far a peripheral issue in the extension scenario will need to be brought centre-stage. Indeed, production will now need to be significantly dictated by market requirements.

Enabling farmers for problem-solving skills

Under the new dispensation, there will be a paradigm shift from top-down blanket dissemination of technological packages, towards providing producers with the knowledge and understanding with which to solve their own location-specific problems. This means that the existing public organizations should improve their efficiency and effectiveness in research and technology application. This will call for an interdisciplinary approach aiming at location-specificity of technical solution.

Encouraging private sector involvement in technology transfer

A significant deterrent to the expansion of private sector involvement in technology transfer is the provision of subsidized agro goods and services by public agencies. This often leads to the creation of an uneven playing field and discourages market entry by private providers. Wherever possible such subsidies will be phased out, in order to stimulate the emergence of a private input supply network to provide hybrid seeds, artificial insemination services, fertilisers, agrochemicals, animal feed, machinery and equipment, and other agricultural supplies and services to farmers on a full cost recovery basis. Generally, the costs associated with the research, development and transfer of these material technologies are embodied in the prices of these products. Therefore, these costs are passed along to farmers, making this component of the Agricultural Technology System (ATS) financially sustainable. Targeted subsidies may be retained to protect the interest of the poor and vulnerable sections. In the field of material technology dissemination, which includes distribution of inputs such as fertilizer, seed, planting material, chemicals for plant protection, agricultural implements etc. a competitive private sector has developed in almost all states except for the north-eastern states. The new policy agenda envisages the withdrawal of the public sector from areas where agro-services can be effectively and competitively provided by the private sector. In such cases, the role of the public sector becomes one of facilitator and enabler. This implies moving towards a realistic cost recovery of agro-services by the State. For, if the public sector continues to subsidize the services, this will prevent a "level playing field" to the private sector, which will ultimately get crowded out. There will need to be a re-examination of existing Rules, Regulations & Acts to abolish provisions, which constrain private investment in the delivery of agro-services.

Public funds for private extension services

Promotion of private extension needs to be matched by corresponding shifts in the allocation of public resources. Public funds would be made available to NGOs, Farmer Associations, Para-professionals or private foundations for extension work. An environment in which private investment in technology generation and transfer is more attractive will, therefore, have to be created.

Charging for extension services

The emergence of a market for private extension advice or consultancy services will be encouraged. Processors with contracted producers, also commercial suppliers of seed, agro-chemicals, machinery, vaccines, artificial insemination and the like should recover the costs of providing advice to their clients out of profit margins. However, the vulnerable group will need to be protected through targeted subsidies and safety nets.

Institutional Restructuring

It is clear that no one uniform extension system will serve as a panacea to all States. Even within States, there will be a combination of various agencies and different institutional arrangements to address the needs of differing agro-climatic zones as well as different sections of farmers. A menu of various models will be available to the States to select and adapt to their own requirements.

Restructuring public extension

Public Extension will continue to remain central to Technology Dissemination, small & marginal farmers & economically backward regions will need to be serviced by it. This implies that public extension functionaries (including VEWs & SMSs) will have to be placed in new decentralized institutional arrangements which are demand-driven, farmer-accountable, bottom-up and have a Farming Systems Approach (broad-based). With supplementation from the private sector, media and Information Technology, the public extension service would be made leaner and professional. It is envisaged that the approximately 100, 000 public extension functionaries will be gradually reduced to be supported by the other two arms of services providers.

District Level Agriculture Technology Management Agency (ATMA) Model

A key concept is to decentralize decision-making to the district level through the creation of the ATMA as a registered society. A second goal is to increase farmer input into program planning and resource allocation, especially at the block level, and to increase accountability to stakeholders. A third major goal is to increase program coordination and integration between departments so that the following program thrusts can be more effectively and efficiently implemented.

Strategic Research and Extension Plans (SREPs) through Participatory Rural Appraisal (PRA)

In the process of creating a more bottom-up extension system, PRA procedures would be introduced across all system levels (district, block, mandal, and village), and across each participating line department and research institutions within the district. On the basis of PRA, Strategic Research Extension Plans would be prepared for the districts. The district SREP must be grounded at the block or mandal level, where extension programs can be fine-tuned to the needs of farmers and more effectively implemented. The SREP would take account of the research, training and extension requirements for production as well as marketing activities. The rural periodic markets and wholesale assembling markets where farmers visit regularly would be used as important locations for the dissemination of market and production technologies.

Block/ Mandal Level Technology Centre for Single Window Extension System

Concept of a Block (or Mandal) Technology Centre (BTC) has emerged wherein a multidisciplinary technology team (comprising block level agriculture, horticulture, soil & water conservation, agricultural marketing and livestock extension officers) would be assigned to organise and implement extension programs within the block. Other line department units and personnel would continue to provide essential service in developmental activities. In effect, the BTC would result in the functional integration of extension activities within the block or mandal and, in effect, become the operational arm of the ATMA. This Centre would become the common meeting point for extension personnel from the line departments to prepare integrated work plans (WPs) and to coordinate their implementation. It would also be the level where farmer input could be more effectively mobilized through a single Farmer Advisory Committee (FAC). The FAC would include 10-12 members representing all major stakeholders within the block. The FAC would help set block extension priorities and recommend resource allocation across program areas. The block technology team would be responsible for operationalizing the SREP in each block and moving toward a single window extension system.

Upgrading and Restructuring the Extension Staff – Field Extension Functionaries as Farm Advisors

The DOA's extension field staff would be restructured and upgraded to create a professional cadre of Farm Advisors. In the process, the village extension worker (VEW) cadre would be incrementally phased out through reassignment and normal attrition. Eventually, these farm advisors would be in charge of all extension activities within the block, and they would all be required to meet a minimum educational requirement for service entry, i.e. B.Sc. (Agri.). In addition, the project would provide in-service training in new planning, diagnostic and technical skills. By the end of this project, this new cadre of extension professionals should be able to identify and provide useful advice for most farmer problems (i.e. become more demand-driven). First, they should be able to carry out a systematic need assessment programme to prioritize farmer problems. Then, by utilizing the strengthened cadre of research and extension specialists (SMSs) within the district, they would be expected to organize and deliver a broader range of extension and farmer training programmes. In addition, these upgraded farm advisors would be expected to formulate and target location-specific recommendations, including systems-based technologies, to reflect the needs of different socio-economic groups of farmers within their block or service area. Besides, the SMS cadre would be expanded and strengthened in the district to support the primary production and farming systems by supplying market-related information to the producers. To facilitate collaboration between the line departments, district-level SMS positions would remain within each development department, but their extension activities would be coordinated under the ATMA framework.

Group Approach to Extension

The contact farmer approach to extension popularised by the T & V is to be replaced by the group approach. Formation and mobilisation of Farmer Interest Groups (FIGs), Farmers Co-operatives and Self-Help Groups will be encouraged with the support of NGOs. Group extension will help to replace the top-down approach with a bottom-up approach in technology transfer, as FIGs will first generate demand for information, technology and management techniques. The extension workers would then respond to the group demand. This would lead to a farmer-extension worker participatory process with emphasis on problem-solving rather than disseminating routine messages. The group approach in an extension would also be in line with the Self-Help Groups of rural credit delivery, water user associations, and co-operatives.

Strengthening research-extension-farmer linkages

There is a need for close interaction between farmers, extensionists and production systems researchers in diagnosing problems together and working out location-specific recommendations emphasizing participation education rather than prescription and joint actions in the field. Accepted to be more knowledge-intensive, these new recommendations will require greater skills both to develop and to apply. There will be strengthening of research-extension-farmer linkages not only at the state and SAU levels but also at the district level; not only between the DOA and the SAUs, but between DOH, DOS and DAH for horticulture, fodder, agro-forestry and Silvi-pasture as well as on-farm land and water management in a farming systems approach with due coverage of agricultural marketing concerns. The research-extension interface at all levels from district to national level will be supported.

Promotion of Multi-Agency Extension Services

Widening the range of extension delivery agencies for the resource-poor farmers and those residing in the hilly, tribal and remote areas, the public system will have to remain as the chief extension mechanism with NGOs possibly being able to play a significant role.

ICAR Role in Extension—Transfer of KVKs to DAC

The primary mandate of ICAR is research. Its extension programmes should be limited to reinforcing the research activities to make them more demand-driven and farmer-centric. Efforts were made towards the end of the 8th Plan to transfer the financial and administrative responsibilities of KVKs to their respective state governments, which could not materialize because of the severe resource constraints faced by the states. Hence, Krishi Vigyan Kendras would continue to operate in pro-active mode, retaining their allegiance with ICAR, for project implementation activities. Apart from focusing on production related issues, ICAR research would adequately address different components of marketing and make available need-based packages in consonance with the changed/changing agricultural marketing scenario. Links with KVKs will be strengthened at the district level through institutions such as ATMAs.

Management Reforms in Agricultural Extension

Central Government Support to State Governments for Extension Services on their Undertaking Policy and Institutional Reforms

After the close of the World Bank-supported NAEP, central support to the state extension services dried up, leaving them with the operation and maintenance of personnel and infrastructure created under T&V. States have barely been able to pay the salaries of extension personnel. Less than 10% of the budget is available for operational expenses, which has practically immobilized the service with scarcely any technology dissemination in the field. It is proposed to support the state extension services provided policy reforms, and institutional restructuring is undertaken with demonstrated ability to be demand-driven, farmer-accountable, sustainable & farming systems based with broad-based integrated delivery. While funding for salaries of public functionaries will continue to be the responsibility of the State Governments, funds for technology dissemination and application (operation & management) would be shared between States & Central Government.

Central Government Funds to be Pooled at ATMA or ATMA like Registered Agencies at District Level

Funds from the central government together with state share for all technology transfer and extension activities would be pooled at these district-level agencies and released for various activities according to the Strategic Research and Extension Plan prepared for the district. At present, annually about Rs. 200 crores worth of funds is released to the states under 100 centrally sponsored schemes (crops, horticulture, inputs, soil & water management) for the purpose of transfer of technology. Wherever ATMAs have been established, they should be the conduits of these funds.

Central Government Assistance to State Agriculture Universities for Expanded Role in Field Extension

On the pattern of the successful scientist-farmer-extensionist model developed by the Punjab Agriculture University, the Directorates of Extension of SAUs would be supported to play a larger role in providing extension services in their service areas.

Central Government Assistance to KVKs

Under the present arrangement, the ownership and mainstreaming of KVKs with the state extension mechanisms have been weak. KVKs, set up as Centres for location specific, adaptive research, if effectively organized to achieve their primary objective of refinement and validation of local technologies could play a strategic role in linking the research and extension systems particularly in the area of farming systems based technologies. It is likely that State Governments will be more willing to own and mainstream KVKs once their relevance as district-level technology refinement institutions integrated with the extension machinery is demonstrated rather than as just another vocational training organization, which they are largely perceived as at present and of which there are several others at the district level.

Promotion of Community –Based Private Extension Services

The group approach is the cornerstone of the restructured extension mechanism. A major component of extension services will be the mobilization of the community into farmers groups - FIGs, FOs, and SHGs. Farmers' Organizations will be linked with Panchayats through existing statutory institutional arrangements such as the Land Management Committees, Development Committees etc. FOs will be supported directly through public funds and will be involved in the planning, implementation, monitoring and feedback of programmes. FOs at the village level would be federated at higher levels. Representatives of FOs would be members of the decision making bodies such as ATMAs, Block level Farmer Advisory Committees, Watershed Associations. The ultimate aim is for FOs to internalize extension services for its members and provide backward (inputs, credit, technology) and forward linkages (post-harvest facilities, markets, value addition) in a vertically integrated arrangement.

Promotion of NGOs based on private extension services

Strength of NGOs is in their ability to mobilize communities into Farmers Organizations/ Farmer Interest Groups/ Watershed Associations/Market Associations. As such NGOs complement the public extension effort in several centrally sponsored programmes. Also, extension services are contracted out and out-sourced to NGOs at the Block level in some states. In such cases, the NGOs substitute for a public extension. Public funds are used to support NGOs and are usually met from the provision of administrative expenses built into the Project Costs. NGOs are also supported directly by the central government in undertaking extension work. Of the 261 KVKs in the country, 86 are operated by NGOs. A systematic training, capacity building and technical backstopping mechanism, supported through public funds are to be developed for NGOs involved in providing extension services.

Promotion of para-professional based private extension

Para-extension workers normally supplement public extension in a relatively cost-effective manner and overcome constraints of absentee public extension functionaries (Gopals for AI services, Mitra Kisan for agri-services such as soil testing etc.). Under the new policy agenda, para-extension workers at the grassroots level will be supported through publicly funded training and capacity building and payment of honorarium in the early years. The honorarium will be routed through the Farmer Organizations/ Farmer Groups serviced by the para-extension workers to ensure accountability to the client group. Once the para-worker is able to demonstrate his/ her usefulness to the client group the honorarium provided through public funds will be phased out, and the client group would take on the onus of paying for the services of the para extension worker. The public extension machinery will also assist para-workers in procuring loans from credit institutions for equipment, mobility and linkages with SMSs in Line Departments and SAUs. There will be an element of partial/ full cost recovery of services provided by para-workers who must ultimately become economically viable units except in the case of vulnerable clients where the State may continue the targeted subsidy.

Panchayati Raj Institutions and extension services

After the 73rd Amendment, most states are conducting regular elections to the Panchayats. Some states have also delegated suitable administrative and financial powers to the three-tier Panchayati Raj institutions. In these states, the extension personnel are placed under the administrative control of the panchayats, whereas for technical guidance, they remain under the control of their respective technical line departments. Since the panchayat systems are evolving in different states and are currently in a state of flux, the ATMA model at the district, the BTCs and FACs at the Block and the FOs at the village level may be organized as conceived, and suitable linkages be forged with the Panchayati Raj Institutions, e.g. the CEO of the Zila Panchayat is the Vice-Chairman of ATMA, the Chairman of the FAC at the Block is the elected chairman of the Development Committee of the Block Panchayat and suitable linkages will be established between various FOs at the village level and the Village Panchayats through the Land Management Committees, Development Committees etc.

Competitive Agriculture Extension Grant Fund

Similar to the Competitive Agriculture Research Grant Fund set up in ICAR and several state governments, wherein both public & private sector research institutions compete for funds to address specific research problems, it is proposed to set up a Competitive Agriculture Extension Grant Fund. Resources under this fund could be accessed through a competitive bidding process. Contracting out extension services to the private sector, community-based organizations or NGOs in selected geographical areas (e.g. a village, cluster of villages, Block) would be done through a transparent, laid out the procedure under this Fund. This would also imply a strict monitoring and evaluation process.

Linkage of performance with funding for public sector

In a manner similar to the private extension agencies who must compete with one another to access funds and whose subsequent eligibility to compete for funds will depend upon their performance as indicated by an independent impact evaluation, it is proposed that on a pilot basis Public extension agencies also be made to compete with private extension agencies for operational funds under Competitive Agriculture Extension Grant Fund (CAEGF).

Contracting out extension support services

Wherever possible extension services in whole or in part could be contracted out for greater cost-effectiveness. This applies, in addition, to administrative services such as security, mobility, computer and secretarial services, participatory planning to NGOs (being done in watershed management), staff training to a University/ Institute, monitoring to a Farmer Organizations/ IIM/ Other Institutions.

Improving Research-Extension Linkages

Promotion of direct interface between farmers and scientists

The direct interface between scientists and farmers is the most ideal and should be undertaken wherever possible. It is an oft-repeated refrain that farmers learn best from scientists or other successful farmers. Moreover, transmission losses are minimized in the direct interface. However, there are relatively high costs attached to this direct mode of technology transfer, and the outreach of scientists is limited. Punjab Agriculture University has achieved significant success through this system. It must be noted, however, that Punjab is a small state geographically and what is applicable to Punjab may not be possible in large states such as Uttar Pradesh, Madhya Pradesh and Maharashtra.

Activating Existing Interface Mechanisms

Regional Committees of the ICAR, Zonal interfaces initiated by DAC, national level pre-kharif and pre-rabi DAC-ICAR interface, state-level bi-annual meetings between line departments and SAUs are all formally instituted mechanisms for improving research-extension linkages. Several of these mechanisms have fallen into disuse or are conducted in a perfunctory manner. As a result, the desired results are not being achieved. These will be activated.

Research priority setting based on SREP

Micro-level extension strategies reflected in the Strategic Research and Extension Plans (SREPs) based on PRA and developed jointly by the district technology teams including the marketing department officials and scientists of the KVKs/ ZRS or SAUs should be formally feedback into the research systems through a research priority setting mechanism in the ICAR.

Capacity Building of Extension Functionaries

Formulation of HRD Policy by States

Central Government support for HRD in Agricultural Extension would be available to the states only after the formulation and adoption of an HRD Policy and Action Plan through a systematic skill-gap analysis (Such a policy would incorporate compulsory training and skill upgradation of all extension functionaries). It would also build in an effective system of rewards and incentives for public extension functionaries.

Formulation of Training Plan for Extension functionaries

A long-term training plan should be developed by each state based on a thorough skill gap analysis. A massive campaign will need to be launched for skill up-gradation and capacity building of extension functionaries using resources of all training institutes. The training is divided into Foundation Courses comprising skill up gradation in:

1. need assessment techniques including the role of participatory rural appraisal
2. group formation
3. development of entrepreneurial skills for agri-business
4. agri-business management
5. WTO and its implications
6. marketing of agricultural produce
7. postharvest management
8. conflict resolution and negotiations between different interest groups

9. management of common property resources
10. use of a different type of media
11. communication
12. project preparation
13. data collection, analysis and documentation.

Foundation courses should be conducted jointly with scientists of SAUs. *Professional Courses* would be conducted at SAUs and Centres of Excellence at the ICAR Institutes in various subject matter disciplines. National and state level agriculture education institutions will need reorientation, keeping in view changing requirements.

One Time Catch-up Grant for Training Infrastructure

One-shot up-gradation of the physical infrastructure of training institutes/ Centres be considered to revive the training institutes to an acceptable level. Funding for this purpose is to be made jointly by the central and State governments.

Upgrading State Level Extension Management Training Institutions

The central government would support State Governments to upgrade and restructure their apex state level training institutions to respond to the changing requirements of extension, training and communication management; these upgraded state level apex institutions could have institutional links with MANAGE/NIAM and function as the state arms of the National level Institute. Structural changes in the form of providing greater autonomy to these State Agricultural Management Extension Training Institutes (SAMETIs) would be a pre-condition of support from GOI. Use of mass media communication techniques will be developed to communicate messages about available technology. Appropriate curricula will be developed for the training of field staff, with a major focus on marketing related issues.

Strengthening Role of MANAGE

The National Institute of Agricultural Extension Management (MANAGE) will be strengthened to enable it to assist the States in developing their HRD capacities.

Developing professionalism in cost effective manner

Training Institutes/ Centres may focus on developing core competency; other services may be outsourced or contracted. Feedback from participants must be used to evaluate the performance of faculty

Training Institutes and SAUs to train private extension functionaries

Facilities of public training institutions and SAUs would be available to NGOs and private extension agents.

Networking among all state-level institutes

All national and state level training institutes will be networked to State headquarters, SAUs and MANAGE. The network will also include private institutions with expertise in different fields.

Empowerment of Farmers

Involving farmers in setting extension agenda

Farmers' representation as major stakeholders will be ensured in all decision -making bodies of public and private extension services. The farmer will be involved in the planning and implementation of extension programmes through formal institutional mechanisms such as ATMAs, FACs etc.

Implementation of programmes through Farmers' User Groups

By ensuring that all programmes in the field are planned and implemented through farmer user groups, such as Watershed Associations, fruit/ vegetable growers cooperatives/ societies, Agricultural Produce Marketing Societies/ Cooperatives etc. farmers would be able to influence both administrative and financial decisions.

Contracting arrangements between governments, extension services and farmers

Contracting arrangements between governments, extension services and farmers, whereby the farmers could play the role of beneficiaries, provider or co-financier of extension services.

Acquisition of Skills by Farmers

Training and acquisition of skills by farmers is a central part of the technology transfer system because of the new practices involved in the production. Greater focus will be provided for (i) assessing farmers' needs and skills; (ii) distinguishing different dimensions of training such as awareness, knowledge, skills and reinforcement, and using appropriate channels and methods for each; (iii) different kinds of technologies and advice required by different categories of male and female farmers, the transfer mechanism (e.g. face-to-face, mass media, different types of groups) they prefer during different phases of awareness, trial and adoption of new skills and technologies (iv) use of information technology for improving the quality and accelerating the transfer and exchange of information; (iv) organising training programmes on system based and sustainable technologies such as Integrated Pest Management (IPM) and Integrated Plant Nutrient management (IPNM); (v) organizing training and taking initiatives for capacity building of farmers towards agricultural marketing. Capacity building, skill up gradation/training of farmers would be largely conducted through farmers' field schools with the active participation of scientists and extension personnel.

Main Streaming Women in Agriculture

Main Streaming women in agriculture

Gender concerns need to be mainstreamed in the agricultural extension process. Public extension systems, which must disseminate new technology and information, are still largely male-dominated. Hence the necessity to target women is to ensure that they receive information relevant to their work, particularly, with reference to crops and livestock.

Improving access to extension and training

Women farmers usually have been neglected in extension efforts. Gender inequality had so far not been challenged by the agricultural extension system in the past. However, with the changing scenario, the need for innovating changes in extension approaches has assumed centre-stage. Under these innovations, efforts will need to be made both by the central and state governments to improve extension services to reach farm women through:

1. Extension policy reorientation that explicitly recognizes farm women as agricultural extension clientele;
2. training of men and women extension staff on women's role in agriculture and rural development and how agricultural extension work could be organized and conducted to meet women's needs in agriculture and rural development activities;
3. training of women on decision-making in the context of farm and home management
4. training of women farmers on agricultural marketing, particularly with respect to post-harvest processing, on-farm value addition and market requirements/demand.

Redesign of extension services to reach women farmers

Extension services are being redesigned to focus on women through:

1. Appropriate training/ sensitization of extension personnel towards the role and contribution of women in the total agriculture system;
2. increasing the proportion of trained female extension workers to gradually ensure that at least one-third of all extension workers are women;
3. sensitising male extension workers to the needs, approaches and perspectives of women through appropriate training and orientation programmes thereby dispelling the notion that only women can address extension needs of farm women;
4. improving communication between women, researchers, marketing agencies and extension workers required for the development of technology suitable for women;
5. developing appropriate extension methodologies that recognize the multi-dimensional role of women and the socio-cultural barriers, in which women farmers operate in rural society;

6. establishing Head of the Farming family as the target group, for extension services and assuming that the information will automatically trickle down to women farmers.

Expanding the sphere of women extension workers

The number of female agricultural extension workers would be increased through:

1. Re-examination of all service cadre rules for hidden gender biases;
2. improvement of female attendance at agricultural institutes and school;
3. building incentives such as scholarships and stipends for more women to take up undergraduate and postgraduate courses in the agricultural and allied sciences;
4. redesigning of agricultural training curricula to include women's concerns;
5. ensuring that women are adequately represented in all training programmes whether domestic or overseas;
6. redesigning of training facilities to make them suitable for large numbers of female students and trainees;
7. inclusion in the teaching curricula for extension workers, greater analysis and extension methods that take into account women's time, mobility and cultural situation; and
8. exploring the specific role of farm women in the marketing of agricultural produce.

Use of Information Technology

Information Technology revolution is unfolding and has very high visibility. However, its benefits have remained confined primarily to the urban areas. Rural communities have not been able to gain to the same extent as IT. As a means of agricultural technology transfer to farmers, information technology, has had a limited impact. Even the vast potential of the broadcasting network has been tapped only minimally for an extension.

Increasing Use of Information Technologies

Harnessing Information Technology for an agricultural extension will receive high priority in the new policy agenda. Extensive use of modern information technology will be promoted for communication between researchers, extension workers and their farmer clients to transfer technologies and information more cost-effectively. Information technology should be made available, particularly, to those with specific inquiries to guide them in adopting the more knowledge-intensive forms of agriculture, which will expand in future.

IT Application in Agriculture Marketing

Agriculture produce marketing requires connectivity between the market and exporters/ growers/ traders, industry consumers, through wide area network of national and international linkages in order to provide day-to-day information with regard to commodity arrivals and prevailing rates etc. to provide links for on-line International market information; to provide export-related documentation, to inform about the latest research in agricultural marketing, packaging, storage-related information and to provide connectivity with lead international and national market organizations.

Wider Use of Electronic Mass Media for Agricultural Extension

Radio and TV have vastly increased their reach, as also reception facilities. "Local" radio and new FM transmitters open up possibilities of area-specific broadcasts. In communicating with an audience with low literacy skills, an audio-visual medium like TV has advantages. Today Doordarshan covers the entire population. Much wider and creative use of the mass media – All India Radio, private FM, Doordarshan, the private cable network will be promoted for more rapid and effective dissemination of general information and advice to farming communities. This will include market information; market-led production planning, on the farm and post-harvest management/value addition, e-contracting, market networks, market intelligence and wider application of the World Wide Web. Face to face contacts should follow and back up these methods of information dissemination, not precede or substitute for them. The central government will support states in their effort to make fuller use of electronic media. The central government would also consider supporting an exclusive Agriculture Channel on Television.

Farmer Participation in IT Programmes

In developing any system of IT for agriculture technology transfer; the farmer is to be kept centre-stage. She/he is not to be treated as a passive recipient but rather as a player, a generator and user of knowledge. The upgradation of his/her skills and knowledge is, therefore, a crucial part of the process. The farmer will be an effective participant in the process.

Support to States for Information Technology

Increased use of information technology at State/ district and block levels would be promoted. This would include electronic access, through NICNET, to technical and administrative information; [e.g. electronic mail (EM) access to ICAR and SAU researchers, plus state and national administrative offices, and electronic access to ARIS system databases and, eventually, to the World Wide Web]. Under the NATP all the Block level Farm Advisory Information Centres in 28 project districts would be electronically linked to the district, state and national institutions. Central Government will support States in the use of electronic linkages and computerization so that marketing, research, extension and farming communities are linked to each other, and into local, national and global networks. The objective is to link all 5200 Blocks to the state and national network and the Internet in a phased manner.

Private Information Shops/ Kiosks

The ultimate aim is to promote private Information shops/ kiosks franchised out to the private sector, especially unemployed rural educated youth, in the manner of PCOs/ STD shops. The private sector will be encouraged to establish information shops at Block/ Mandal/ Village level. A major programme for the development of software will need to be mounted so that Information Shops could have access to suitable material. Electronic connectivity and access to e-mail would put the franchisees in contact with district KVKs, Line Departments, markets and other sources of information. Such information could be dispensed to farmers, farmers groups on payment. Credit facilities for the purchase of equipment for setting up such Information Shops would be permissible under the micro-credit programme for agriculture and allied activities.

Capacity Building for the use of IT

Application of IT is constrained by lack of or inadequacy of complementary inputs (equipment, power, etc.), appropriate organisational and institutional structures, information management and skills development. A major training programme for developing the capacity for IT usage will be promoted. Training Institutes will run suitable courses for the purpose.

Financial Sustainability & Resource Mobilization

Publicly funded extension will continue to play a predominant role in technology dissemination firstly because the large numbers of small disadvantaged farmers may not have access to or be able to afford any other kind, and secondly, because much of the new technology will not be commercially marketable for instance watershed management, land capability assessment and land use planning, breaking of yield ceilings sustainable management of natural resources and socio-economic research. But pressures on government expenditure mean that public funds will have to be more carefully targeted and more efficiently used.

Cost-cutting mechanisms for extension services

Cost-effectiveness may be improved by relying on fewer but better qualified (graduate or postgraduate) field advisers who interact directly with researchers for subject matter advice and then multiply their impact in the field by working with farmer groups rather than individual contact farmers. Cost cutting mechanisms, including the exploitation of mass media, encouragement of NGO and private sector involvement in extension, or needs-based coverage

Efficient use of available resources

Optimum fund utilization will be achieved with better matching the farmers need with extension delivery, a stronger focus on the economics of farming, and the use of participatory methods to assess needs, create a commitment to action, and monitor impact.

Privatization of agro-services

An environment in which private investment in technology generation and transfer is more attractive will be created. Product diversification both horizontal and vertical shall be promoted to not only improve profitability sustainability and more efficient use of production resources but also to encourage greater involvement of the private sector. Where opportunities exist to contract out publicly-funded services or to transfer costs to the corporate sector or to users themselves, these opportunities should be exploited-for instance for diversification into higher-value or export crops, or to develop new commercial inputs or machines. Privatization of selected "private goods" and agro services wherever a competitive market exists, such as AI services, soil testing, fertilizer advice, farm improvement plans or breeding plans would be undertaken. Wherever feasible contract farming through thc involvement of the private sector would be taken up, particularly, in the area of high value/ export-oriented agriculture.

Towards a realistic cost recovery of agro-services

Wherever farmers have the capacity to pay for public services, which are in the nature of private goods, the realistic cost of such services should be recovered. However, provision is made for targeted subsidies to protect the vulnerable class of users.

Co-financing of public extension

Co-financing of public extension services by farmers and farmers' associations to reduce pressure on public finances and to improve the accountability and responsiveness of extension to farmers.

Initiating new financial systems

Modification in rules and regulations and innovations in financial institutions will also be required to allow for arrangements such as "revolving funds" for government farms, nurseries, etc. While budgetary support to these units may continue to meet pay and allowances of government staff, the funds for recurring expenditure and operational costs could be generated by these units from the commercial activities undertaken by them. All efforts would be made to develop credit linkages of farmers and farmers groups with credit institutions.

Changing role of Government

Role of State in Effective Regulation & Enforcement

As a multi-agency extension regime proliferates, the responsibility of the State for effective enforcement of legislation, which ensures quality control of inputs such as seed, pesticides, fertilizers etc. will increase. State's role as arbitrator of conflicts between various private sector extension agents will also increase, and systems to address grievances will need to be developed. This role will increase as the number of private extension agencies grows. Guidelines for private agencies would be required. However, in the emerging pluralistic scenario, the role of the public extension would need to be redefined from one of solely a provider of services to become increasingly an appropriate mix of provider, coordination, facilitator and regulator. The large section of small and marginal farmers and landless labourers, as well as remote and backward regions, would continue to need the services of the public extension functionaries, as they are not likely to be serviced by a competitive private sector in the near future. Public Extension's role would increase in the arbitration of conflicts, assuring accountability of all service providers to the farmers and ensure transparency through provision of information. The overall environment of private provision of extension services deserves to be encouraged through policy reforms and institutional changes, so that rural people's needs serviced more efficiently.

Creating an Enabling Environment

Generally, this implies appropriate legislation, rules and regulations, and application of the rule of law. In particular, it implies that private contracts and property are protected and a judiciary exists to enforce contracts without partiality and undue delay. Where many individuals smallholders are concerned a legal course of action may, however, not be practical or politically expedient for handling conflicts and disputes. The government can instead support institutions like an independent arbiter, an ombudsman, or a small farmer reference service that would certify bona fide borrowers or agricultural producers. Governments can also set minimum standards and norms for commodities such as food, pesticides, and packaging materials when it is in the interest of public health. To protect the weaker of the contracting parties, governments can propose minimum standard contract clauses and guidelines for small farmer/ agribusiness transactions. It is essential that such proposals be seen as recommendations, not prescriptions. An important condition for lasting farmer-agribusiness linkages is the security of tenure. Activities supported by international donors in many countries include land titling, the formal transfer of public land to de facto users, and outright land reform.

Enhancing Competition

The enhancement of competition is another government contribution to improving the institutional environment. It involves all measures to ensure open, fair and transparent competition and to facilitate entry of newcomers. It may include breaking up of monopolies and cartels, ensuring minimum professional standards of business conduct, and resisting demands for non-technical obstacles to official licensing by rent-seeking lobbies. A lack of financial means is frequently the reason that prevents newcomers from establishing new businesses. Governments can assist young entrepreneurs in accessing credit and venture capital by providing technical assistance to prepare business plans, conduct market surveys and hire help to resolve special engineering or legal problems and through this to improve the confidence of funding sources in new ventures. Part of creating an enabling environment would also be to address the downside of privatization and liberalization. This might include the provision of safety nets and skills for alternative livelihood to those who are unable to survive the competition in deregulated markets.

Strengthening Farmers' Associations

Government services can help identify existing associations or cooperatives of farmers and support them to develop their organization. The aim must be to assist the groups in defining their objectives, such as savings mobilization or specific post-harvest operations, to ensure group coherence and continuity, and to assist them with setting up group structures and organization. Over time such groups can establish a track record of organizational maturity that will allow, possibly after joining with other groups for economies of scale, to engage in their own business activities and to gain access to formal credit. Government extension services and NGO staff need to receive suitable training to act as group facilitators. Training would be centred on group dynamics, record keeping and accountancy, financial management of savings and credit, identification of group business opportunities and producing business plans, and on imparting technical skills to undertake new ventures. Support to farmers' organizations is perhaps the main single input that governments can provide for the promotion of farmer integration with agribusiness.

Strengthening Physical Infrastructure

The government's role would increasingly be in the area of physical infrastructure provision, including communications and utilities, farm-to-market roads, and rural and urban markets. Promotion of the private sector would be through making available sites with road and electricity connections to attract enterprises that may set up marketing or processing facilities as part of an industrial estate. Rural or farm-to-market roads also facilitate linkages between farmers and private service providers. Similarly, the development of wholesale market yards is also supported by governments at given stages of marketing development. At more advanced stages such facilities tend to lose their functions, as alternative forms of marketing development for a variety of agricultural products that rely on direct producer/ agribusiness/ consumer linkages and by-pass traditional markets.

Improving Information

Another way of levelling the playing field for the private sector is the improvement of information. Information gathering and analysis is costly. Compared to commercial business, farmers are at a disadvantage on knowledge about prices, volumes, qualities, alternative marketing channels and other feature governing market transactions. The government can improve the communications flow, and the quality of information to farmers through training workshops and publications and by this improve transparency and facilitate transactions. The government can also sponsor market-matching exercises, that is, sponsor meetings and workshops involving farmers and agribusiness enterprises to improve mutual understanding of constraints and requirements, and promote concrete business deals.

Conclusion

Through their sheer numbers and outreach, the public extension system would continue to play a prominent role in technology dissemination. The large section of small and marginal farmers and landless labourers would need to be serviced by the public extension systems. The other actors involved in the extension/ transfer of technologies such as NGOs, Farmers Organizations, Private Sector (both corporate & informal), para-workers etc. would actively complement/ supplement the efforts of the public extension agency and wherever possible replace it. Extension mechanisms will have to be driven by farmers' needs, be location specific and address diversification demands. Technologies required to address total farming systems are knowledge intensive. Public extension system will need to be redefined with a focus on knowledge-based technologies to upgrade and improve the skills of the farmers.

As agricultural extension transforms itself into a more diversified farming systems approach from its present simplistic accent on yield enhancement by increasing some limited inputs, farmers will be required to adopt a wider range of inputs and practices and develop skills in their more efficient use. The task of the extension will become more challenging in the wake of the post-WTO era, which demands a system of market-led extension with a specific focus on diversification, post-harvest management and export orientation. This will present a more complex role but simultaneously requiring a flexible approach allowing specific information to be customized for different farmer-groups. A strategy of institutional innovations in extension will be evolved, which optimizes the strengths of the public-private sectors to service the needs of the farming community.

(Source: http://agricoop.nic.in/policy_framework.htm)

14.2 NATIONAL AGRICULTURE POLICY OF INDIA

The first ever National Agriculture Policy was announced on 28th July 2000. The National Policy on Agriculture seeks to actualise the vast untapped growth potential of Indian agriculture, strengthen rural infrastructure to support faster agricultural development, promote value addition, accelerate the growth of agro-business, create employment in rural areas, secure a fair standard of living for the farmers and agricultural workers and their families, discourage migration to urban areas and face the challenges arising out of economic liberalization and globalisation. Over the next two decades, it aims to attain:

- A growth rate in excess of 4 per cent per annum in the agriculture sector;
- The growth that is based on efficient use of resources and conserves our soil, water and biodiversity;
- Growth with equity, i.e., growth which is widespread across regions and farmers;
- The growth that is demand driven and caters to domestic markets and maximises benefits from exports of agricultural products in the face of the challenges arising from economic liberalization and globalisation;
- The growth that is sustainable technologically, environmentally and economically.
- The policy seeks to promote technically sound, economically viable, environmentally non-degrading, and socially acceptable use of the country's natural resources - land, water and genetic endowment to promote sustainable development of agriculture.
- The use of bio-technologies will be promoted for evolving plants which consume less water, are drought resistant, pest resistant, contain more nutrition, give higher yields and are environmentally safe. Conservation of bio-resources through their ex situ preservation in Gene Banks, as also in situ conservation in their natural habitats through bio-diversity

parks, etc., will receive a high priority to prevent depletion of biodiversity.

- Balanced and conjunctive use of biomass, organic and inorganic fertilizers and controlled use of agrochemicals through integrated nutrients and pest management (INM & IPM) will be promoted.
- A regionally differentiated strategy will be pursued, taking into account the agronomic, climatic and environmental conditions to realize the full growth potential of every region. Special attention will be given to the development of new crop varieties, particularly of food crops, with higher nutritional value.
- A major thrust will be given to the development of rainfed and irrigated horticulture, floriculture, roots and tubers, plantation crops, aromatic and medicinal plants, bee-keeping and sericulture for augmenting food supply, promoting exports and generating employment in the rural areas.
- Development of animal husbandry, poultry, dairying and aquaculture will receive a high priority in the efforts for diversifying agriculture, increasing animal protein availability in the food basket and for generating exportable surpluses.
- An integrated approach to marine and inland fisheries, designed to promote sustainable aquaculture practices, will be adopted.
- The regionalization of agricultural research based on identified agro-climatic zones will be accorded high priority. Application of frontier sciences like biotechnology, remote sensing technologies, pre and post-harvest technologies, energy saving technologies, technology for environmental protection through national research system as well as proprietary research will be encouraged.
- The research and extension linkages will be strengthened to improve the quality and effectiveness of research and extension system.
- Adequate and timely supply of quality inputs such as seeds, fertilizers, plant protection chemicals, bio-pesticides, agricultural machinery and credit at reasonable rates to

farmers will be the endeavour of the Government.

- The Government will endeavour to create a favourable economic environment for increasing capital formation and farmer's own investments by removing distortions in the incentive regime for agriculture, improving the terms of trade with manufacturing sectors and bringing about external and domestic market reforms.
- Rural electrification will be given a high priority as a prime mover for agricultural development. The quality and availability of electricity supply will be improved, and the demand for the agriculture sector will be met adequately in a reliable and cost-effective manner.
- Bridging the gap between irrigation potential created and utilized, completion of all on-going projects, restoration and modernization of irrigation infrastructure including drainage, evolving and implementing an integrated plan of augmentation and management of national water resources will receive special attention for augmenting the availability and use of irrigation water.
- Emphasis will be laid on the development of marketing infrastructure and techniques of preservation, storage and transportation with a view to reducing post-harvest losses and ensuring a better return to the grower.
- Setting up of agro-processing units in the producing areas to reduce wastage, especially of horticultural produce, increased value addition and creation of off-farm employment in rural areas will be encouraged.
- Institutional reforms will be pursued so as to channelise their energies for achieving greater productivity and production.
- The Government will provide active support for the promotion of a cooperative form of enterprise and ensure greater autonomy and operational freedom to them to improve their functioning.
- The endeavour will be made to provide a package insurance policy for the farmers, right from the sowing of the crops to post-harvest operations, including market fluctuations in the prices of agricultural produce.

- The price structure and trade mechanism will be continuously reviewed to ensure a favourable economic environment for the agriculture sector and to bring about an equitable balance between the rural and the urban incomes.
- Quality consciousness amongst farmers and agro-processors will be created. Grading and standardization of agricultural products will be promoted for export enhancement. Application of science and technology in agriculture will be promoted through a regular system of the interface between Science and Technology institutions and the users/potential users to make the sector globally competitive.
- The database for the agriculture sector will be strengthened to ensure greater reliability of estimates and forecasting, which will help in the process of planning and policy making.

Follow up Action

Various Central Sector and Centrally Sponsored Schemes are being implemented by the Government of India and the State Governments for development of agriculture and allied activities as per guidelines of the Agriculture Policy. Following major initiatives have been taken to accelerate the pace of developmental activity and implement the objectives of the Agriculture Policy:

- Macro Management Scheme has been launched after integrating 27 ongoing Centrally Sponsored Schemes to enable a shift from programmatic approach to a macro-management mode of assistance to the states in the form of work plans based on crop/area specific, regionally different strategies, to provide flexibility to State Governments and to ensure timely and effective application of limited financial resources.
- Common guidelines have been issued for the National Watershed Development Project for Rainfed Areas to harmonize the implementing norms with other watershed development programmes. A Watershed Development Fund, with a corpus of Rs.200 crores each from NABARD and the Department of Agriculture & Cooperation, has been created.
- A Technology Mission for the Integrated Development of Horticulture in the North-Eastern Region has been launched.

- Seed Legislation is under revision to provide a fillip to varietal research and plant breeding. Enactment of legislation on the "Protection of Plant Varieties and Farmers Rights". This is likely to stimulate investment and initiative both in public and private sector for the development of new plant varieties and vibrant seed industry. A National Seed Policy is under formulation. A Scheme for Seed Crop Insurance has been launched to cover the risks involved in seed production. A Seed Bank has been established to meet contingent requirements of seed in the wake of natural calamities.
- Increasing availability, flexibility and security in the flow of credit to the farmers. All eligible farmers are proposed to be covered under the Kisan Credit Cards scheme within the next 3 years. A personal insurance package is proposed to be extended to Card Holders covering them against the risk to life and injury.
- A scheme has been introduced for provision of capital subsidy for construction/modernization and expansion of cold storages and storages for horticultural produce.
- Rural Infrastructure Development Fund corpus was increased in 2001-02 from Rs. 45,00,00,00 thousand to Rs.5,00,00,000 thousand and the interest rate charged by NABARD reduced.
- Market Information Network has been launched with the objective to provide farmers with the latest information on price movements of agricultural commodities and other essential data.
- Cooperative Sector Reforms: a new Bill has been formulated and introduced in Parliament for replacing the existing Multi-State Cooperative Societies Act, 1984.
- Formulation of new subsidy linked scheme for the establishment of rural godowns.
- Promotion of Food Processing Industries and value addition in agriculture through the excise exemptions and other interventions.
- Standing Committee of Union Ministers and Chief Ministers constituted to consider issues concerning agricultural strategies, food management and promotion of agriculture

exports. The Committee has approved the outline of the proposed Grain Bank Scheme which will be extended to BPL families in identified areas and developed on the contours of the recently launched Sampoorna Grameen Rozgar Yojana.

(Source: http://agricoop.nic.in/agpolicy02.htm)

Bibliography

Benor, D and Baxter, M (1984) Training and Visit Extension. The World Bank, Washington

Bhatnagar, O.P. and Desai, G.R. (1987). Management of Agricultural Extension: Concept and Constraints, National Institute of Rural Development, Hyderabad.

Bloome, P. (1993) Privatisation Lessons for U.S. Extension from New Zeland and Tasmania. Journal of Extension, Spring.

Chambers, R., (1983). Rural Development: Putting the Last First. Longman, London

Chandra Shekahr, P. (2001) Private Extension in India; Myths, Realities, Apprehensions and Approaches. MANAGE, Hyderabad

Communication for Development. Oxford & IBH publishing Co. Pvt. Ltd. New Delhi

Coombs, P.H. and Ahmed, (1974) Attacking Rural Poverty: How Nonformal Education Can Help. The Johns Hopkins University Press, Baltimore

Dahama (1965) Cited in Dahama, O.P. and Bhatnagar, O.P. (1991) Education and Communication for Development. Oxford & IBH publishing Co. Pvt. Ltd. New Delhi.

Dahama, O.P. and Bhatnagar, O.P. (1991) Education and Communication for Development. Oxford & IBH publishing Co. Pvt. Ltd. New Delhi.

David, G. and Ken, K (1990) Small farmer, Big Business. Contract farming and Rural Development. Mc Millan, London.

Dayal, P (1993) Broad Basing of Agricultural Extension. Agricultural Extension Review Vol 5(2)

Ensminger (1962) cited in Dahama, O.P. and Bhatnagar, O.P. (1991) Education and Communication for Development. Oxford & IBH publishing Co. Pvt. Ltd. New Delhi.

Ensminger, D (1957). A Guide to Community Development. Ministry of Community Development and Cooperation, Govt of India, New Delhi.

Etling, A.W; Radhakrishna, R. B. and Bowen, B. E. (1993) Participatory Planning and Decision Making in Agriculture, in Extension Strategy for Agricultural Development in 21st Century (ed) R.K. Samanta, Mittal Publications, New Delhi

Horton, M (1962). Extension Philosophy. In Spirit and Philosophy of Extension Work (eds) R.K. Bliss *et. al.* Graduate School, USDA, Washington.

IGNOU (1990) Rural Development, Block 2 of Rural Development: Indian Context. IGNOU, New Delhi.

IGNOU (1992) Rural Development Administration. Block 3 of Rural Development: Indian Context. IGNOU, New Delhi

International Cooperation Administration (1957) Community Development Guidelines. Community Development Review, 3.

Kelsey, L.D. and Hearne, C.C. (1954) Comparative Extension Work. Comstock Associate, New York

Kelsey, L.D. and Hearne, C.C. (1967) Cooperative Extension Work. Cornell University Press, New Delhi

Kokate, K. D. Kharde, P.B, Patil, S.S. and. Deshmukh, B.A (2009) Farmers'- Led Extension: Experiences and Road Ahead, Indian Res. J Ext. Edu. 9 (2), pp 18-21.

Leagans, J.P., (1961). Characteristics of Teaching and Learning in Extension Education, Extension Teaching Methods, The Communication Process and Programme Planning to Meet people's needs, in Extension Education in Community Development, Directorate of Extension, Govt of India, New Delhi.

Lininger, F.F. (1953) The Importance of Agricultural Extension and the Possibilities of International Cooperation. In IASC and AUW (1953) Methods of Agricultural Extension.

MANAGE (2007) Course 101, Introduction to Agricultural Extension Management, Block II, New Dimensions in, Agricultural Extension, National Institute of Agricultural Extension Management, Hyderabad

MANAGE (2008) AEM 201, Market-Led Extension, Block I, Basics of Market-Led Extension, National Institute of Agricultural

Extension Management, Hyderabad

Mandal, S. and Roy, G.L. (2007). Textbook of Rural Development. Kalyani Publishers, Ludhiana

Ministry of Community Development and Cooperation (1962). A guide to community Development, Govt. of India, Calcutta

Misra, D.C. (1990) Defining Agricultural Extension for the 1990s. Directorate of Extension, Govt. of India, New Delhi.

Mukharjee, B. (1967) Community Development in India. Orient Longmans, Bombay.

National Commission on Agriculture (1976) Report, Part I, Review and Progress and Part XI, research education and Extension, Ministry of Agriculture and Irrigation, Govt. of India, New Delhi.

Ramesh, T (1999) Contract farming and Vertical integration in Indian Agricultural Sector: An Overview. Seminar Report, Submitted to the Department of Agril. economics, UAS, Bangalore.

Ray, G. L., (1996). Extension Communication and Management. Naya Prakash, Calcutta

Roling, N. (1982) Alternative Approaches to Extension, In Progress in Rural Extension and Community Development (ed) Jones and Rolls. Cited in Misra, D.C. (1990) Defining Agricultural Extension for the 1990s. Directorate of Extension, Govt. of India, New Delhi.

Rudramoorthy, B (1964) Extension for Planned Social Change, Allied Publishers Pvt. Ltd. Bombay

Sandhu, N. (1998) Corporatisation of Agriculture Needed. Tribune (17.10.1998) in Agricultural News. Vol. 4 (5) National Academy of Agricultural Science New Delhi.

Sarvanan, R and Gowda, N.S.S. (2003) Contract Farming: Where We Gain and Lose? Manage Extension Research Review. Jan-June.

Schwartz, L. (1994) The Role of Private Sector in Agricultural Extension, Economic Analysis and Case studies. Agricultural Research and Extension Network. Paper No 48. Overseas Development Institute, London

Singh, A. K. (2001) Contractual Arrangement in Land Markets in Rural Areas. *Indian Journal of Agricultural Economics.* Vol. 56(1).

Singh, K. (1986) Rural Development: Principles, Policies and

Management. Sage Publication, New Delhi.

Singh, S. (2005) Changing Structures and Organisation of Agriculture and Small Farmers in India. Social Change. Vol. 35(4).

Swanson, B.E. and Claar, J.B. (1984) The History and Development of Agricultural Extension. In Agricultural Extension: A Reference Manual (ed) Swanson, B.E., FAO, Rome.

Taylor, C.C., Ensminger, D. Johnson, H.W and Joyce, J (1965). India's roots of Democracy. Orient Longmans, Bombay.

United Nations (1956) Community Development and Related Services. Community Development Review, 3.

van den Ban, A.W. and Hawkins, H.S. (1988) Agricultural Extension. Longman Scientific and Technical, England

van den Ban, A.W. and Hawkins, H.S.(1996) Agricultural Extension. Blackwell Science Ltd, Oxford.

Wijkoom, R.R.A (2003) Concept Paper presented to Sri Lanka Council for Agricultural Research Policy

ONLINE

http://agro.indiamart.com/agro-programme-schemes/ http://india.gov.in/sectors/agriculture/index.php

http://bicol.da.gov.ph/News/2005news/2qtr05/flc.html

http://megindustry.nic.in/citizen2.htm

http://nfsm.gov.in/

http://webmani.nic.in/techmission/TechnologyMission.htm, http://india.gov.in/sectors/agriculture/tech_mission.php

http://www.authorstream.com/Presentation/nikesh_saye-739349-market-led-extension-122847298998928l-9/

http://www.indg.gov.in/hi/agriculture/tribal-areas/agri-tribal-itdaroles http://www.nmdfc.org/pdf/18.pdf

http://www.indg.in/agriculture/rural-employment-schemes/national-horticulture-mission/nhm-guidelines-english.pdf

http://www.indg.in/agriculture/rural-employment-schemes/nfsm-operational guidelines.pdf

http://www.indg.in/agriculture/rural-employment-schemes/nfsm-operationalguidelines.pdf

http://www.sociologyguide.com/women-and-society/mahila-samridhi-yojana.php http://agri.gujarat.gov.in/download/rkvy.pdf

Jones, G.E. and Garforth, C. (1997) The History, Development and Future of Agricultural Extension. In Improving Agricultural Extension, A Reference Manual (ed) Swanson *et. al.* Online http://www.fao.org/docrep/W5830E/w5830e03.htm

Sharma, V. P[1] (2005) "Cyber Extension: Leveraging the Inforevolution to Improve Rural Livelihoods- Case Studies in Agricultural Extension *ww.csdms.in/conflux/Proceedings05/.../ VP_Sharma.pdf*

Sharma, V.P[2] (nd) http://www.gisdevelopment.net/proceedings/mapasia/2003/papers/i4d/ i4d003.htm

SIL International (1999) Formal versus non-formal education. On line http://www.sil.org/ingualinks.literacy/prepareforaliteracyprogram/FormalversusNonformalEducation.htm

www. dcmsme.gov.in/publications/pmryprof/ABOUTPMRY.html

www. rmk.nic.in/chap1.htm

Index